GUIDE
TO
INDIVIDUAL AND FAMILY
FINANCES

Adrian Fellows

Editor Roger Sproston

D0588480

Straightforward Guides
www.straightforwardco.co.uk

Straightforward Guides

ISBN :
978-1-913342-56-2

Printed by 4Edge Ltd www. 4edge.co.uk

Cover design by BW Studio Derby

Whilst every effort has been made to ensure that the information
contained within this book is correct at the time of going to press,
the author and publisher can take no responsibility for the errors
or omissions contained within.

CONTENTS

Ch. 13-Sources of Pensions-A Summary   184

**

INTRODUCTION

The main purpose of this book, **updated to 2020** is to guide the reader through the maze of personal financial decisions which he or she or the family might have to make during a lifetime. Currently, we are in a period where the COVID 19 pandemic is dominating our lives and playing havoc with the economy. Peoples incomes are being affected and returns on investments (for the most part), have been decimated. Savings rates have dropped right down and there is even talk of negative interest rates. That is why it is now so important to understand the opportunities available.

In addition, Britain's exit from the European Union may well affect different parts of the financial landscape. This is a case of wait and see.

I have concentrated heavily on specific areas such as pensions, savings and insurance, because these are areas which have been affected the most and which will have the most effect on you during the course of your working life. The book also discusses the operations of the stock market and how to invest wisely. There are also frequent references to financial advisors, ranging from the independent advisor to those employed by institutions such as banks. I have made repeated references because very often you will receive advice from such a person and will make decisions based on that advice. It is very important indeed to know exactly who you are receiving advice from.

As an individual, you could spend untold hours considering the various options open to you with regard to financial matters, only to find yourself more confused than ever due to conflicting advice received along the way. That advice will, quite often, be made in the best interests of the advisor, and his or her subsequent commissions, rather than in the best interests of yourself.

A Guide to Individual and Family Finances will set out, in a clear and unambiguous way, the meaning and implications of the various financial options open to you, and should leave you in a better position to make an informed choice.

The main areas covered by the book are mortgages, life insurance, savings generally, investments, income protection, stocks and shares, tax wills and trusts and pensions. In addition, I have also covered education, and health care plus wedding and funeral plans. Because of the importance of receiving accurate advice from financial advisors, the book will begin by outlining the law that governs such advisors and also the types of advice given.

**

Ch. 1

Financial Advice/ Financial Advisors

There are many ways to purchase financial products nowadays, either through the Internet or by telephone. However, when considering more complex financial issues, it is evident that professional advice is needed. There are numerous advantages to using financial advisors, one of the main ones being that you will have extra protection if things go wrong. The first step towards finding a good advisor is considering which type is likely to provide the service you need. Like solicitors and other professionals, financial advisors do specialise and you would have to find the correct advisor for your needs. It is also very important to discover whether or not the advisor is properly authorised and registered and approved by the correct bodies. Nowadays, advisors and the companies that they work for must be authorised by the financial services watchdog, the Financial Conduct Authority (FCA). The FCA is responsible for the conduct of advisors. To be on the safe side you should always check with the FCA. You can also find out what type of business the advisor is authorised to do. These details are held on the FCA's register. Its public enquiries helpline is on 0800 111 6768. It is important to be aware of the distinctions between different types of advisors, the services they are likely to provide, and how they are likely to be paid, before narrowing your choice down.

Different types of investment advisers

Financial advisers come in different guises and aren't always called 'financial advisers'.Sometimes they are named by their specialism such as 'mortgage adviser', 'investment adviser', 'pension adviser' or 'financial planner'. Sometimes they are known as 'brokers' - often when dealing with products like home and car insurance, mortgages or investments like shares.

Advisers who deal with: Investments; pensions; retirement income products (such as annuities) and general financial planning

Since January 2013, advisers recommending these types of products must charge a fee for the advice they give and carry higher levels of qualifications. Prior to this, many were paid by commission collected from charges on the products they sold.

In reality, advisers who provide advice on the products listed above, might also provide advice on protection insurance (such as life insurance) and sometimes mortgages. Many offer holistic financial planning, where they will advise you on all aspects of your financial needs. Advisers in this category are classified as either independent or restricted.

Independent financial advisers can recommend all types of retail investment products from firms across the market. **Restricted** advisers might either be restricted in the type of products they offer, or the number of providers they choose from. Make sure you understand the type of service they offer before you decide whether to get advice from them. You should choose an adviser who can deal with a wide range of product providers for the product they are recommending – and not just one or two.

That way you know you will be getting the widest choice.

Advisers who deal with: Mortgages and equity release

Mortgage advisers must have specific mortgage qualifications. Advisers recommending equity release products must also have a specialist qualification in equity release. These advisers are still permitted to be paid by commission on any mortgage or equity release product they sell. Some mortgage advisers also charge a fee for their services. Many mortgage advisers can also advise on protection insurance such as life insurance.

Mortgages advisers might offer a whole of market service, although this won't necessarily mean they can recommend any mortgage from every lender as some lenders only offer mortgages direct to the public. Some mortgage advisers are tied to just one lender or might only be able to choose from a small number. So an adviser who offers a whole of market service will give you the widest choice.

Advisers who deal with: General insurance products (such as home, car and travel insurance)

These advisers are often also known as insurance brokers. Like mortgage advisers they are paid by commission on any insurance product they sell, but don't normally charge an additional fee. Insurance brokers will also help you deal with any claims you might make and will shop around for you every year to make sure you're getting the best deal.

If your circumstances are out of the ordinary- for example if you live in an area susceptible to flooding or you have health issues and need travel insurance - an insurance broker can be especially useful. They know the insurers who deal with your type of insurance need and will be able to find you the best deal.

However, some insurance brokers will have a wider range of providers that they deal with than others so always check the level of service they offer and how many providers they work with.

As with other types of financial advice, brokers who deal with a wide range of insurance providers will give you the widest choice.

Other types of 'advice'

If you are only given general information about one or more investment products, or have products or related terms explained to you, you may have received 'guidance' rather than 'advice'. This is sometimes also called an 'information only' or 'non-advice' service. The main difference between guidance and advice is that you decide which product to buy without having one or more recommended to you. Buying an investment product in this way might reduce the cost involved but it also means you might not have access to the Financial Ombudsman Service or Financial Services Compensation Scheme (FSCS) if things go wrong. The rules around the compensation scheme may change after the UK leaves the EU on 31st December 2020.

If you are not sure whether you are receiving guidance or advice, and therefore how you would be protected, you should ask the adviser or firm to explain.

Fees and charges

A financial adviser can help you make the most of your money but you need to be confident you are getting advice that is right for you. there have been improvements in this area.

The Financial Sector Conduct Authority ("FSCA") previously known as the Financial Services Board ("FSB") implemented the RDR in December 2012, to, amongst other things, help ensure that customers are treated fairly when purchasing financial products. RDR is linked to the Treating Customers Fairly ("TCF") framework, TCF being a principles based framework and the RDR providing some of the rules associated with that framework. RDR is intended to be implemented in 3 phases, with the first phase having commenced on 1 January 2018.

1. Know how much advice costs

Advice has never been free. If you received financial advice before the changes you were probably paying commission to your adviser. Commission was usually a percentage of your investment – typically 1% to 8%, or sometimes more on a lump sum. So for an investment of £10,000, your adviser could have received between £100 and £800 commission.Instead of you paying commission on new investments your adviser now has to clearly explain how much advice will cost and together you will agree how you will pay for it. This can be a set fee paid upfront or you may be able to agree with your adviser that they can take their fee from the sum you invest. This way you know exactly what you are paying and that the advice you receive is not influenced by how much your adviser could earn from the investment.

2. Know what you are paying for

Financial advisers can either advise you on all products that may be right for you or focus on certain areas, such as pensions.

Following the changes, financial advisers that provide 'independent' advice now have to consider all types of investment areas. They can also consider products from all firms across the market. An adviser that has chosen to offer 'restricted' advice can only consider certain products, product providers or both. Your adviser has to clearly explain what they can advise you on.

3. Get improved professional standards

Some investments can be hard to understand. So the FCA have increased the minimum professional standards of qualification that advisers have to meet, to ensure their knowledge is up to date.

What you should do next

Next time you see your adviser ask how much you have been paying for their advice and how much that same advice now costs. Your adviser should be able to explain how these changes affect you and your finances, and whether they offer independent or restricted advice.

The Money Advice Service offers clear guidance relating to the use of financial advisors www.moneyadviceservice.org.uk.

Services offered by other advisers
Accountants

Accountants are usually the best source of advice on tax matters. Some can also advise on investments provided that they are authorised by the FCA. Some of the larger accountancy forms have specialist independent financial advice departments to provide a full planning service. You will have to pay a fee to accountants for such advice but any commission generated by sales of products is usually offset against the final bill.

For names of local accountants contact the Institute of Chartered Accountants, the Association of Chartered certified

Accountants or the Chartered Institute of Taxation and Association of Tax Technicians (see appendix).

Actuaries

Actuaries are normally employed by insurance companies but there are also firms of independent consultants who can be approached for specialist advice on insurance related matters such as pension transfers. They work on a fee basis. The Association of Consulting Actuaries can provide you with the name of a firm in your area.

Banks and building societies

Most larger banks and building societies have in-house financial consultants who are tied agents. In the future, some banks may become multi-tied and start offering the products of several companies but their range will still remain limited. Some banks offer advice through private arms designed for wealthier customers (with more than £100,000 to invest for example).

Company representatives

Many insurance companies have their own sales forces to promote their products and services. Traditional insurers, such as Legal and General and the Co-operative still employ hundreds of representatives who will visit people in their own homes to discuss their needs. Companies selling direct by telephone also use their own representatives.

Solicitors

If you need legal advice on certain matters such as dealing with wills and probate, you will need to consult a firm of solicitors. They may also be able to provide financial planning and investment advice on a fee basis. There are two organisations that represent solicitors offering these services. They are the Association of Solicitors and Investment Managers (ASIM) and Solicitors for Independent Investment Advice. If you have a legal problem relating to a pension, you should contact the Association of Pension Lawyers. See appendix for details.

Stockbrokers

Stockbrokers have become more accessible over the years, particularly recently. Many of the newer telephone based services cater mainly for investors who know which shares they want to buy and sell, and they do not provide advice other than general information bulletins. However, many firms still offer advisory and discretionary management services. For smaller investors, a unit or investment manage trust management may be offered.

To find out which stockbrokers offer these services to private clients, contact the Association of Private Client Investment Managers and Stockbrokers (APCIMS). It has a free directory of member firms, many of which provide a full financial planning service. See appendix for details.

Tied agents

Tied agents are also known as 'appointed representatives'. These are self-employed consultants or companies, which have a contract to sell one or more of an insurance company's products or commission. The agent may operate independently in respect of other business. For example, many building societies are tied agents and will sell the investment and investment products of one insurance company.

Online Advisor Directories

Online advisor directories are a vital resource and can help you to locate a financial advisor suited to you and the type of advice you might need. The main online directors are Vouchedfor and Unbiased but there are others from the personal finance society and the aforementioned Money Advice Service as well as more specialist lists from the Society of later Life Advisors and findawealthmanager.com. Services are free for consumers but advisors can pay for referrals.

Complaints

If you are unhappy with a financial product or service, you have the means to complain. As with many complaints, you must first give the company the chance to put things right. If this cannot be achieved then there are other routes, such as the Financial Ombudsman Service.

However, before the Ombudsman will take up your complaint you must be able to show that you have followed the company complaint procedure and have still received no satisfactory solution to your problem.

Complaints schemes generally

The Financial Ombudsman Service. This provides a single complaints scheme divided into three specialist divisions for banking and loans, insurance and investments. It covers the following types of companies and organisations:

- Banks
- Building societies
- Financial advisors

- Firms dealing in futures and options/ Friendly Societies
- Fund managers
- Life insurance companies
- Pension providers
- Stockbrokers

The Pensions Advisory Service. PAS provides initial advice and conciliation for complaints about employers pension schemes.

The Pensions Ombudsman. This ombudsman decides on complaints relating to employers pension schemes not resolved by OPAS.

The General Insurance Standards Council. This is a voluntary scheme handling complaints about general insurance brokers such as those selling motor and household cover.

The Property Ombudsman Scheme. This is a voluntary scheme dealing with complaints about estate agents from both buyers and sellers. All estate agents are required to register with some sort of Estate Agents Redress Scheme approved by the Office of Fair Trading..

Protection

If you lose money due to miss selling or misadministration, an ombudsman may be able to ensure that you get financial compensation. However, if fraud is apparent, this may not be possible, or if the company or individual becomes bankrupt.

The Financial Services Compensation Scheme

The maximum amounts of compensation are as follows:

Deposits

£85,000 per person per firm

100% of first £85,000

Investments

£85,000 per person per firm

100% of first £85,000

Home (e.g. Mortgage advisors and arrangements)

£85,,000 per person per firm

100% of first £85,000

Pensions

If the firm failed after 1st April 2019 you will be paid 100% of your claim with no upper limit. If your SIPP provider fails up to 85% of your claim is paid per individual per firm. If you have received bad pension advice you could be eligible to win compensation up to 85% per person per firm.

Insurance business

If you bought your insurance policy from an insurance firm that's failed, and you bought your insurance after 8th October 2020 the kind of insurance you have and when the firm failed will affect how much compensation you could claim.

100% protected:

Compulsory insurance

Long-term insurance

Professional indemnity insurance

Claims arising from the death or incapacity of the policyholder due to injury, sickness or infirmity

Building guarantee policies

90% protected:

All other kinds of insurance

There are different rules for insurance purchased before October 2020 and for further advice on all compensation schemes you should go to the Financial Services Compensation Scheme website at fscs.org.uk.

Fraud Compensation Fund run by the Pension Protection Fund

This covers member liabilities of occupational pensions in full.

Offshore compensation

Investors should bear in mind that these schemes do not apply to firms based outside the United Kingdom. Although some offshore investment centres, such as the Isle of Man, may have their own compensation schemes, others do not. When investing outside the UK take great care to gain as much information as possible from the institution concerned.

**

Ch. 2

Mortgages and Financing a Property Purchase

Most people purchasing a property will need a mortgage. There were many products on the market and deposits were not always required. Following the onset of the pandemic however, the mortgage market has tightened considerably and mortgage providers are not that willing to accept low deposits due to the volatility in the housing market True, at the time of writing there has been a temporary rise in house prices due to changes in stamp duty rates, but this is seen by many mortgage providers has a false dawn. below, we discuss some of the hurdles put in place following COVID 19.

The hidden mortgage hurdles

Borrowers who have recently opened a current account, got a new credit card or been given a deposit for a home by their parents are being hit by hidden blocks on mortgages. Banks and building societies, some of whom fear a house-price crash, have been accused of stifling the market with rules aimed at reducing the number of risky borrowers on their books. First-time buyers with small deposits and self-employed workers are bearing the brunt of the measures, which have often been introduced with no warning. Lenders are taking steps such as:

- Declining to lend to borrowers with deposits given by relatives.
- Refusing loans for purchases of flats for those with a small deposit

- Banning borrowers who recently shopped around for a new credit card
- Refusing to include bonuses in approval calculations
- Barring workers who have been furloughed, or those industries that have had significant job cuts

Nearly 1.9 million mortgage holidays have been agreed since March, according to UK Finance, the trade group for the banking sector. While many have since restarted repayments, there are fears about borrowers' ability to repay in the future. On top of that, in the worst-case scenario, house prices are expected to fall sharply next year, leaving many people, particularly those who had small deposits, in negative equity – where their home is worth less than the amount they owe on a mortgage. According to Lloyds Bank, 106,985 people moved home in the first six months of the year, a 31 per cent decline compared with the same period in 2019 – the biggest drop since the 2008 financial crisis. Fist-time buyer numbers declined 29 per cent to 11,843.

HSB has said that it would not grant mortgages on flats unless borrowers had at least a 15 per cent deposit. For new-build flats this rises to 20 per cent. The threshold was previously set at 10 per cent. The bank also imposed extra requirements on interest-only mortgage, for which borrowers have to prove they have a plan in place to pay back the loan when it ends. If their repayment plan involves a stocks and shares ISA, HSB will now take into account only 50 per cent of its value, which must have been calculated in the past 35 days. This move is down to market volatility in the wake of the pandemic. TSB recently barred new customers from getting a mortgage if they have taken out three financial products in the past six months, including current accounts, credit cards and loans including, for example, interest-free credit for furniture or a car loan. NatWest is now requiring all self-employed workers to have a discussion with a business manager to explain whether Covid-19 has affected their income before they submit an application. The market is changing very quickly. Nationwide has warned that two, five and ten-year fixed-rate deals were about to go up by 0.5 percentage points, giving borrowers. Lenders are also wary of certain professions they think will be at risk of job losses due to coronavirus – including retail workers airline pilots and chefs. Landlords are facing similar restrictions. TSB has said buy-to-let borrowers can get a mortgage only if the property they rent has an energy efficiency rating of E and above., while Barclays has stopped lending to portfolio landlords – those who have four or more buy-to let mortgaged properties – in a move it says is aimed at managing the level of applications it is getting. The Bank of Mum and Dad has been curtailed by lenders, with Nationwide now requiring anyone applying for a 10 per cent deposit mortgage to have saved at least three quarters of the deposit themselves. Anyone relying on commission or bonuses to shore up their income will not be able to borrow as much money; Bank of Ireland and Post Office Money, for example, recently said they would not accept bonuses when deciding how much money to lend. Those who have kept up their mortgage and other loans repayments throughout the pandemic, and have not opened too many credit cash cards in the past few months, are most likely to be accepted by a lender. Even if a borrower has been furloughed, if they can prove they are due to return back to work they are more likely to be accepted. In this case, lenders might ask for a letter from the employer confirming they are going back full-time.

Financial advisers will give you plenty of advice but not always the best advice. Sometimes, particularly now, it is better to go to the lender direct. Before you talk to lenders, work out what your priorities are, such as tax advantage, early repayment and so on. Make sure that you are aware of the costs of life cover. The below describes mortgages generally and what types of lenders there are.

Lenders-Banks and building societies

There is little or no difference between the mortgages offered by banks and building societies. Because banks borrow against the wholesale money markets, the interest rate they charge to borrowers will fluctuate (unless fixed) as and when their base rate changes. Building societies however, which will rely more heavily on their savers deposits to fund their lending, may adjust the interest rate charged for variable mortgages only once a year. This may be a benefit or disadvantage, depending on whether rates are going up or down.

Centralised lenders

Centralised lenders borrow from the money markets to fund their lending and have no need for the branch network operated by banks and building societies. Centralised lenders, which came to the fore during the 1980s, particularly the house price boom, have been criticised for being quick to implement increases but slow to implement decreases, through rate reductions. This is, simply, because they exist to make profit. Therefore, you should be cautious indeed before embarking on a mortgage with lenders of this kind.

Brokers and "independent" financial advisors

In chapter one, we discussed financial advisors. Brokers act as intermediaries between potential borrowers and mortgage providers. If they are "tied" agents they can only advise on the products of one bank, insurance company or building society. If they are independent they should, technically, advise and recommend on every product in the market place.

A word of warning. It is up to you to ask detailed questions about any product a broker offers you. You should ask about fees. If possible, you should arrange a mortgage direct with a bank and avoid so called independent brokers.

How much can you borrow?

There is a standard calculation for working out the maximum mortgage that you will be allowed. For one borrower, three times annual salary, for a joint mortgage, two or two and a half times combined. Lenders, however, will vary and some will lend more. Be very careful not to overstretch yourself. As stated, banks and building societies have tightened up their lending criteria, following the onset of CIVID 19, and mortgages are hard to obtain without hefty deposits. The Financial Conduct Authority have introduced tough new rules to ensure that no one can borrow more than they can afford to repay. Under the new rules, interest only mortgages will only be offered to people with a firm and clear repayment plan, rather than simply relying on the rise in house prices to cover repayment of the capital. Lenders will also have to take account of future interest rate increases on repayment costs.

Mortgage Market Review

New rules came into force in April 2014 means that those seeking a mortgage should brace themselves for a long wait to see a mortgage adviser, three-hour interviews at the bank and forensic analysis of your daily spending habits.

Even after jumping through all those hoops, success is not guaranteed – experts have warned thousands of buyers and home owners are likely to be rejected because they do not meet the new requirements.

The City regulator, the Financial Conduct Authority (FCA), has introduced the new rules, known as the Mortgage Market Review, to ensure borrowers are issued with mortgages they can afford both now and in the future. The FCA was concerned that lenders were making it too easy to get a mortgage before the financial crisis. Many households borrowed too much money and found they were unable to keep up their repayments when the financial crisis struck.

So-called "self-cert" loans, where borrowers declared their income but did not have to prove or "certify" it, were common and people routinely exaggerated earnings to borrow more. Interest-only loans also caused problems. Borrowers flocked to these deals because their monthly repayments were lower, but they had no way to repay the capital at the end of the loan.

To ensure safer lending in future, mortgage providers are now responsible for assessing whether customers can afford the loan in the long term. This includes buyers and those who are remortgaging and want to increase the size of the loan, vary the time frame or transfer it to a new property.

Deposits

Most banks and building societies used to lend 95% maximum, some more than that. However, for now, those days are over. Lenders will usually require higher deposits. The best source of information for reputable lenders is in the weekend newspapers. However, still, the more that you put down the better deal that you are likely to get from the lender. There are a number of websites which offer comparisons. one such site is Which? www.which.co.uk/money. There are numerous other comparison sites.

Help to buy ISA

We will be discussing ISA's further on in the book, but the Chancellor introduced a Help to Buy ISA in the 2015 budget, which came into effect in Autumn 2015. The Help to Buy ISA closed to all new accounts from 30th November 2019. If you have already opened a HTB ISA or did so before 30th November 2019 you will be able to continue saving in to your account until 30th November 2029.

These HTB ISA's applied to first time buyers over the age of 16. For every £200 saved in this ISA the government deposits £50. This means that when £12,000 has been saved the government will contribute an extra £3000. This is to be used towards a deposit and can be claimed when buying a property. The bonus will be available on homes costing up to £450,000 in London and £250,000 elsewhere. For more information you should go to: www.helptobuy.gov.uk/help-to-buy-isa.

Help to Buy equity loans

Some homebuyers will have more time to buy their home if they reserved it by 30 June 2020. They must have experienced severe delays with their purchase due to COVID-19. To find out more go to Help to Buy: Equity Loan customers during Coronavirus (COVID-19). A new Help to Buy: Equity Loan scheme open to first-time buyers only will be available for two-years from 1 April 2021. The Help to Buy scheme will end on 31 March 2023.

A Help to Buy equity loans are only available to people who want to buy a new build property. They work like this:

The government lends you up to 20% of the property's value as an equity loan;

-You'll need a deposit of at least 5%;
-You'll need to get a mortgage of 75% of the property's value.

So if you wanted to buy a house worth £200,000, it would break down as:
-A £40,000 loan from the government;
-A £10,000 deposit put down by you;
-A £150,000 from a mortgage lender.

The benefit to getting an equity loan from the government is that with a larger amount to put down, you'll hopefully get a better mortgage rate from your lender. For more information on this scheme you should go to www.helptobuy.gov.uk/equity-loans.

Equity loans - what you'll have to pay back
-The equity loan is interest free for the first five years;
-From the sixth year onwards you will pay an admin fee;
-The admin fee will start at 1.75% of the loan;
-The admin fee will increase every year by any increase in the Retail Prices Index plus 1%.

Remember, you will be paying these fees in addition to your mortgage repayments and the equity loan from the government will not be decreasing in size (unless you opt to repay part of it early). So, over time the cost of the admin fee could become pretty expensive. You will need to repay the equity loan in full after 25 years, when your mortgage term finishes or when you sell your home - whichever happens first. You will repay the market value of the loan at the time, rather than a fixed cash amount. In practice, this means:

-You take a 20% equity loan to buy a property worth £200,000, or £40,000;
-When you sell the property, it's worth £250,000;
-You repay £50,000 - this is 20% of the new value of your home, not the amount you borrowed;
-If the property had dropped in value, you'd pay less than you borrowed.

You can also choose to repay part of the loan early in chunks of either 10% or 20% of the total value.

Joint mortgages
How do joint mortgages work?
You could get a larger mortgage if you buy a home with someone else.

What is a joint mortgage?
You can buy a property with one or more other people by getting a mortgage in the names of both or all of you. Everyone named on the mortgage will be responsible for making repayments. You can decide between you how you share the equity in the property. This is the percentage of it that you own, which increases as you pay off more of the mortgage.

Who can get a joint mortgage?

Joint mortgages are usually taken out by couples. They are available to married couples, unmarried couples and civil partners.

However, you could also buy a home with:

- One or more friends or family members you intend to live with
- A friend or family member who wants to help you afford a property or buy part of one as an investment
- A business partner who wants to invest in property with you

Most joint mortgages are taken out by two people, but some lenders will allow up to four people to buy together.

How much can you borrow with a joint mortgage?

You can usually borrow more if you buy with someone else because your combined income will be higher than what you earn alone. If both of you have a regular income, you will be able to afford a more expensive property than you could on your own. Lenders used to multiply your income by a set amount to decide how much they would lend you. For example, they might have offered three times your combined income. If you earned £30,000 and your partner earned £20,000 a year, they would lend you up to £150,000.

However, they now base it on a more advanced calculation that takes into account your income, your credit record and what you spend each month on bills and other expenses.

How much do joint mortgages cost?

They come with the same costs as standard mortgages, including interest and mortgage fees. However, if you can save a higher deposit between you, this should give you a better choice of mortgages, so you could choose one with a lower interest rate than if you bought a property alone.

How to get a joint mortgage

The process of making a joint mortgage application is the same as applying on your own. However, you and the person you are buying with will need to do the following together:

- Make decisions
- Fill in and signing application forms
- Meet mortgage advisers or solicitors

How does joint ownership work?

Everyone named on a joint mortgage is equally responsible for making sure the full repayment due is made to the lender each month. You may decide to split the payments 50/50, but if the other borrower stopped paying their half, the lender could pursue you for the missing money. If you want to make any changes to your mortgage like borrowing more or changing it to a new fixed rate deal, this will have to be authorised by all of the borrowers. There are two ways you can each own your property with a joint mortgage:

Joint tenants

Take out a mortgage as joint tenants if you want all of the borrowers to legally be seen a single owner and to have equal rights in the property. Owning the property equally as joint tenants is usually used by long term couples. If one borrower died, the other borrowers would inherit their share of the property· If you sold the property, any profits would be split among you all equally. If you re-mortgage the property, you will need to get a new mortgage together, not separately

Tenants in common

Taking out a mortgage as tenants in common lets you all own legally separate shares in the property. This is usually used when friends, family members or business partners buy a property together. The shares you each own can be for whatever percentage you choose and do not have to be split evenly. You can sell your share in the property separately. You can leave your share of the property to someone else in your will. For example, if you bought a property worth £150,000 with one other person and you owned 60% of it, your share would be worth £90,000 once the mortgage has been paid off. A solicitor can draw up a deed of trust, which is a legal document that specifies the percentage of the property you each own.

Joint mortgages will affect your credit report

If you apply to borrow money in the future, lenders will run a credit check when they decide whether to accept you.

The following could show on your credit record if you have a joint mortgage:

1.

A financial association with the person you buy with. This person will be linked to you on your credit record, so if they have bad credit it could affect what lenders think of your ability to meet repayments.

2.

Borrowing money shows on your credit report, and the amount of debt you have will influence whether lenders think you can afford to borrow more.

3.

Missed or late payments show up too and are likely to put off potential lenders.

Can a joint mortgage be split?

Yes, you can get out of a joint mortgage, but it can be complicated in some circumstances. You can either sell the property and share the money you get from it, or one person could buy the other's share in the property.

Main types of mortgage-
Endowment

With this type of mortgage, you have to take out an endowment insurance policy which is then used to pay off the mortgage loan in a lump sum at the end of the term. There are a number of different types designed to achieve the same end:

- Low cost with profits. This is the usual sort of endowment, guaranteeing to pay back part of the loan only. However, because bonuses are likely to be added, it is usually enough to pay off the loan in full;
- Unit linked endowment. With this, the monthly premiums are used to buy units in investment funds. The drawback is that there is no guarantee how much the policy will be worth on maturity, since this depends on how well the investments have performed.

A word of warning. Endowment products were pushed heavily by financial brokers. There was an obsession with them in the 1980's. This is because they earn big commission for those people that sell them. Like a lot of salespeople, motivated by greed salespeople, some advisers failed to reveal the down side. This is:

-Endowments are investment linked and there is no guarantee that they will have matured sufficiently at the end of the term to repay the mortgage. This leaves you in a mess. A repayment mortgage will definitely have paid off the mortgage at the end of the term. If you change your mortgage and decide that you do not wish to continue with an endowment mortgage, and so cash in the policy early you will almost certainly get a poor return unless it is close to maturity. In the early years of the policy, most of your payments will go towards administration and commission (a fact that your broker does not always reveal). The alternative in these circumstances is to maintain the endowment until it matures, treating it as a stand-alone investment which will, hopefully, make you some money eventually.

Repayment mortgages

This mortgage, where the borrower makes regular repayments to pay the mortgage off over the term is a fairly safe bet. However, if you plan to move house every five years then this will not necessarily be the best mortgage for you. With a repayment mortgage, you pay interest every month but only a small proportion of the capital, particularly in the early years of the mortgage. An endowment mortgage, while more risky, could be better for you under these circumstances, since you can transfer the plan from property to property, while it can, hopefully, grow steadily as it matures.

Pension mortgages

Similar to the other products except that the payments go into a personal pension plan with the remainder after paying the mortgage forming the basis of a pension. The same characteristics apply as to the others.

Interest only mortgage

The borrower pays interest only on the loan, and decides how he or she will pay the loan off at the end. The lender will want to know this too, particularly in the light of the new rules introduced, mentioned above.

Mixed mortgages

A new development is that one or two lenders now allow borrowers to mix a combination of mortgages in one deal, customising the mortgage to suit each individual.

Foreign currency mortgages

Some foreign banks offer short-term mortgages in the foreign currency of that bank. Their lending criteria can be much more relaxed than trying to borrow from a British lender. The advantage of this sort of mortgage depends on currency fluctuations. If the pound is stable or rises, the borrower benefits. If the pound drops, the borrower will have to pay more.

These types of home loans should be left to more sophisticated investors as there is the potential to get into trouble unless you have a clear grasp on the implications of such a mortgage.

Cashbacks

You probably saw the adverts offering large sums of cashback if you took a particular product. If you read the small print, unless you took the highest mortgage available with the highest deposit then you would not get anywhere near such a sum. This mortgage was typical of the many mortgages on offer in the pre-credit crunch times. You would be very hard pushed to see such an offer now.

Other types of mortgage

Given the state of the property market at the current time, it's not surprising that the 'bank of mom and dad' is increasingly being called on to help find the large deposits needed by their offspring, particularly in the south of England where property prices are grossly distorted and more and more people are paying sky high rents, on top of everything else.

One mortgage that has grown in popularity is the Joint Borrower Sole Proprietor Mortgage (JBSP) which have grown in popularity since the government removed stamp duty for a large proportion of first-time buyers. These specialist mortgages take the income of two borrowers into account, typically a parent or child, but only puts the child's name on the property deeds. This avoids the stamp duty that a property owning parent would incur if their name was on the deed because, since 2016, there has been a 3% stamp duty surcharge on second homes.

To be eligible, borrowers need to be closely related, for example parent and child rather than uncle and nephew. A number of banks, such as Barclays and the Bank of Ireland offer these sorts of mortgages but each have their own terms and conditions concerning income variables.

What to do if you feel that you have been given wrong advice

The mortgage lending market is very complicated and many people have suffered at the hands of financial advisors and others who have given incorrect advice. Mortgage regulation has not been very tight. However, the basic framework is as follows:

- Sales of mortgage linked investments like endowments or pensions are regulated by the Financial Conduct Authority. Anyone selling investments must be qualified and registered and must be able to clearly demonstrate that the policy that they have recommended is suitable. All registered individuals and firms are inspected by regulators and can be fined or expelled from the industry if guilty of wrongly selling products.
- By contrast, information on mortgages is currently regulated by the industry only, voluntarily, under a code of mortgage practice sponsored by the Council of Mortgage Lenders. Although most of the big players are signed up to the code there are still some who are not. Check first before taking advice.

How to complain

- Complain first to the company that sold you the product, going through its internal complaints procedure.
- If you are unhappy with the firm's decision, approach the relevant complaints body. For mortgage advisors employed directly by lenders, or complaints about lenders generally, contact the Financial Ombudsman

Service on 0800 023 4567 or online www.financial-ombudsman.org.uk

- For mortgage lenders which are not building societies or banks but which are signed up to the mortgage code, the Chartered Institute of Arbitrators 020 7421 7444 www.ciarb.org will assist.
- If your complaint is about a mortgage broker, contact the Chartered Institute of Arbitrators which may be able to help if the firm is registered under the code.
- Complaints about endowments, pensions and other investments is handled by the Financial Conduct Authority 0800 111 6768 www.fca..org.uk and are dealt with by the financial ombudsman Service.

The most common complaint is to do with endowments. A lot of people bought products which they came to regret. They are a major source of profit to the provider-and all those in between-but the person left holding the problem is the consumer.

If you believe that you have been given bad advice about anything to do with the insurance or investment side of a product then you should approach the Financial Services Authority.

The Building Society Association or the British Bankers Association have free publications that should help you. In addition, the Consumers Association, "Which" runs regular articles on mortgages. Remember - always ask questions. Never rush into anything. Always take advice if you are uncertain. Banks and building societies themselves are usually a better source, a safer source than individual advisers.

Borrowing and the internet

Almost all lenders have their own sites and many operate internet only loans with keener rates than those available on the high street. But there are also growing numbers of mortgage broker sites, offering mortgage calculators so that you can work out how much you can afford to borrow and how much the true cost of your loan will be.

The following are a selection of independent sites:

www.moneysupermarket.co.uk
This is an online mortgage broker with a choice of over 4000 variable, fixed rate, capped and discounted mortgages as well as more specialist loans for right to buy, buy to let and self build property, also self certification loans.

www.moneynet.co.uk
This is an independent on line mortgage broker, offering mortgages from over 100 lenders. Again, as with all these sites it will provide a clear and comprehensive picture of mortgages available and is easy to use, just follow the instructions.

What is stamp duty and who pays it?

Stamp Duty — Stamp Duty Land Tax (SDLT) official jargon — is a tax you pay when you buy a home. The buyer pays stamp duty – not the person selling.

There are different rules if you're buying your first home.

Residential property rates

You usually pay Stamp Duty Land Tax (SDLT) on increasing portions of the property price when you buy residential property, for example a house or flat. SDLT only applies to properties over a certain value.

The amount you pay depends on:
- when you bought the property
- how much you paid for it
- You must send an SDLT return if you pay more than £40,000 for a property - even if there's no SDLT due. There are some exemptions.

Rates from 8 July 2020 to 31 March 2021

You can use the table below to work out the SDLT for the purchase price of a lease (the 'lease premium').

Up to £500,000	SDLT % Zero
The next £425,000 (the portion from £500,001 to £925,000	5%
The next £575,000 (the portion from £925,001 to £1.5 million	10%
The remaining amount above £1.5 million	12%

Example In March 2021 you buy a house for £625,000. The SDLT you owe will be calculated as follows:
0% on the first £500,000 = £0
5% on the remaining £125,000 = £6,250
total SDLT = £6,250

Rates from 1 April 2021

These rates also apply if you bought a property before 8 July

2020.

You can use the table to work out the SDLT for the purchase price of a lease (the 'lease premium').

Up to £125,000	SDLT % Zero
The next £125,000 (the portion from £125,001 to £250,000	2%
The next £675,000 (the portion from £250,001 to £925,000	5%
The nest £575,000 (the portion from £925,001 to £1.5m	10%
The remaining amount (The portion above £1.5m)	12%

Example In May 2021 you buy a house for £275,000. The SDLT you owe will be calculated as follows:

0% on the first £125,000 = £0

2% on the next £125,000 = £2,500

5% on the final £25,000 = £1,250

total SDLT = £3,750

If you're buying your first home. You can claim a discount (relief) if you buy your first home before 8 July 2020 or from 1 April 2021. This means you'll pay:

- no SDLT up to £300,000
- 5% SDLT on the portion from £300,001 to £500,000

You're eligible if you and anyone else you're buying with are first-time buyers. If the price is over £500,000, you follow the rules for people who've bought a home before.

New leasehold sales and transfers

When you buy a new residential leasehold property you pay SDLT on the purchase price of the lease (the 'lease premium') using the rates above. If the total rent over the life of the lease (known as the 'net present value') is more than the SDLT threshold), you'll pay SDLT at 1% on the portion of net present value over:

- £500,000 for purchases from 8 July 2020 to 31 March 2021
- £125,000 for purchases from 1 April 2021

This does not apply to existing ('assigned') leases.

Higher rates for additional properties

You'll usually have to pay 3% on top of SDLT rates if buying a new residential property means you'll own more than one.

You may not have to pay the higher rates if you exchanged contracts before 26 November 2015.

If you're replacing your main residence

You will not pay the extra 3% SDLT if the property you're buying is replacing your main residence and that has already been sold. If you have not sold your main residence on the day you complete your new purchase you'll have to pay higher rates. This is because you own 2 properties. You can apply for a refund if you sell your previous main home within 36 months.

There are special rules if you own property with someone

else or already own a property outside England, Wales and Northern Ireland. If it takes longer than 36 months to sell your previous main home You may still be able to get a refund of the extra 3% SDLT if:

- you purchased your new home on or after 1 January 2017 the delay was outside your control, for example because of coronavirus (COVID-19) or a public authority blocking the sale
- you have now sold your old home

To claim a refund, write to HMRC and explain why the sale took longer than 36 months.

Special rates
There are different SDLT rules and rate calculations for:

- corporate bodies
- people buying 6 or more residential properties in one transaction
- shared ownership properties
- multiple purchases or transfers between the same buyer and seller ('linked purchases')
- purchases that mean you owe more than one property
- companies and trusts buying residential property

Solicitors' fees
A solicitor has to be appointed to act on your behalf and also of the relevant lender. All lenders have a panel of acceptable solicitors and you should check to make sure that you are using a firm that is acceptable otherwise you could be expected to pay two sets of fees.

Your solicitor will carry out various checks and searches and will make numerous enquiries with the owner's solicitors about any issues you or the lender may need to have clarified before you commit yourself.

Based on a purchase price of £275,000 the fees payable to your solicitor would be approximately: £2000 approx plus vat inclusive of disbursements but excluding stamp duty.

Illustration of Solicitors' Fees and Disbursements
Purchase price   £275,000
Legal fees:
Solicitors conveyancing fees £2000
Stamp Duty   Zero (Until 1st April 2021)
Local Authority search fee   £180 approx.
Land Registry fee   £140 approx.
Land Registry search fee   £10
Bankruptcy search fee   £1 per client
Other searches such as contamination and water and sewerage etc £200
Total £2531

The most important part of the initial cost is, of course, the deposit money. This is now going to be as much as you can afford, at least 10%, due to the banks unwillingness to take risks. This money must be from your own savings or a gift from family etc. because if you are borrowing the money it is effectively a 100% loan.

The deposit money is paid to your solicitor on exchange of contracts as this is the time of the transaction when you totally commit yourself to the property. You would normally move in two or three weeks after.

Advice for parents helping children on to the property ladder

In spite of the many incentives now on offer to help young people onto the property ladder, prices are still way too high for most people. There are a number of ways for parents to help their children, outlined below.

Help with the deposit

A 'gifted deposit' is one way to help children. Most lenders will want to see a letter from parents confirming no future interest in the property. A gift is also a way to avoid any future inheritance tax liability, assuming that you survive for more than seven years after the money has been gifted.

Saving early

If you have the foresight you should think of saving early for children's deposits through junior ISA's which have an annual limit of £9,000 from April 2020/2021.

There are a number of other ways to help, such as remortgaging your home and also offsetting family savings.

**

Ch. 3

Life Insurance

The concept of life insurance is by no means a 20th century development. The earliest forms can be traced back to Greek and Roman times. Clubs would be formed and, for a regular contribution, a lump sum would be paid in the event of death of an individual.

In today's society, we are expected to insure for virtually everything and anything and at the end of the month there are normally limited funds to insure for the most important issue, YOU.

Do you need it?

Many people feel they do not need life insurance. In some cases this is true but the vast majority have families and feel that they need to be protected in the event of an unexpected death. It is not always the main income provider who needs all the life cover. Provisions must be made if there are children and the non-working parent spends his or her time looking after them. The cost of employing a child minder or even giving up your full time job must be considered. This could be easily remedied with a basic life insurance policy.

If you have a mortgage the banks and building societies normally insist that you have the relevant life insurance to cover the mortgage debt and in the case of endowment mortgages the life insurance forms part of your endowment premiums, but with repayment mortgages the cost of premiums is extra.

As you are probably aware, if you haven't got any life cover other than in conjunction with your mortgage then you are likely to be under-insured. If you are in an occupational pension scheme you are likely to have cover as part of your benefits. This would normally work out to be 3 times your basic salary and if you have a personal pension plan you can have life cover up to 3 times and you would receive tax relief on your premiums.

To establish how much life cover you require you need to calculate how much income the family needs to survive each year. Take away any state benefits you would be or are entitled to and then multiply this figure by the number of years your youngest child has before he or she leaves school.

Example

A family requires £15,000 per year income.

No benefits available.

The youngest child is 9. Therefore there is a minimum of 7 years before the child could leave school and start work.

7 x 15 = £105,000 life cover

You could say that the life cover quoted would be too much after the first year, but the youngest child could always go on to sixth form or college and may not actually start work until he or she is 20 years old.

Different types of life insurance

Most forms of life insurance are paid on a monthly or yearly premium basis. The premium you pay will purchase a level of cover and it can be on a fixed or variable term. There are a multitude of insurance policies geared to the individual's needs and requirements, and we will now look at the differences.

Decreasing Term Assurance

This policy is commonly known as mortgage protection and is normally used in conjunction with a repayment mortgage. As we have already discovered with a repayment mortgage the debt reduces further throughout the term and the same can be said about the decreasing term insurance. The amount of life cover will decrease in line with the mortgage. This policy can be written in joint names and is the cheapest form of life assurance available. There is no investment value to this contract and in the event of a claim, the benefits are payable to the estate.

Example

Mortgage Protection Assurance

Male non-smoker age at entry not exceeding 30
Female non-smoker age at entry not exceeding 30

Benefits
Initial sum assured   £50,000
Plan Term   25 years

Monthly cost
Premium payable for 25 years
or until first death if earlier £9.57
Warning - the contract has no cash-in value at any time.

Level term insurance

This policy works on the same basis as the above, but the life cover will not reduce as the term goes on. For this reason, the premiums are slightly more expensive.

Family income benefit policy

This policy will simply provide an annual income for your dependents instead of a lump sum. This is a good way too ensure that the provisions that you have made are not used up in one spending spree. Once again, this contract can be written in joint names, but has no investment value.

Whole life

This type of policy is considered to be the most flexible contract in the life insurance market. Unlike the other contracts this policy does have investment value and it is not written on a fixed term. The amount of cover you require can be altered at any time to suit changes in your personal circumstances. The premiums you pay are not fixed and are reviewed every 5-10 years to establish whether the insurance cover can still offer you the level of cover for the premium you are paying. This policy is quite expensive in comparison to term policies. It is, however a great deal more flexible and it can be written in joint names.

Example
Whole of Life min/max cover basis

Male, non-smoker, age 30 next birthday
Female, non-smoker, age 30 next birthday
Amount of Life Cover payable on first death:
minimum   £10,350
maximum   £114,900
Monthly premium   £25

Critical illness

A new innovation in the insurance industry is the introduction of critical illness insurance.

Surveys have shown that more people are concerned about being diagnosed as having a critical illness than they are of dying. The implications of having a major illness are immense as you could find yourself stuck with the financial commitments but without the income and ability to pay them. The introduction of critical illness means that if you are diagnosed with any of the defined illnesses in the contract, you will receive a lump sum. The amount of the lump sum depends on your premiums and your age. The benefit of critical illness means that you can afford private medical treatment or afford to pay off your debts. Below are listed the main conditions that are considered to be critical illness:

-multiple Sclerosis--heart attack--kidney failure--loss of a limb
-stroke--major organ transplant—cancer—Coma--benign brain tumour
-severe burns

This is not a technical guide or a total list of definitions. It is simply a selection of some definitions. Critical illness can be taken out by itself, or as part of a whole life or endowment. Critical illness does not have investment value. It can be written in joint names.

Example
Male, non-smoker, age next 30 next birthday
Female, non-smoker, age 30 next birthday
Initial monthly premium   £25.00
Initial sum assured   £65,000
Life Assured basis   joint life, first event
Cover type   Maximum

The premium is payable until the earlier of the:
- death of the last to die of the lives assured.
- diagnosis of one of the lives assured suffering a critical illness.

The premium will increase annually by the amount required to support the increase in benefits as a result of the Automatic Increase Option.

What the benefits might be

The greater of the sum assured and the encashment value of the plan will be payable on the diagnosis of one of the lives assured suffering a critical illness.

**

Ch. 4

Maximising Your Savings

The fact that interest rates have gone down drastically at the time of writing, 2020, means that people are now having to look very carefully at where they save their money in order to get the highest return.

People save for a number of different reasons, dependent on their circumstances and on age. Some people save in order to have enough to help their children and others save for a prosperous old age. Whatever the reason, it is important to understand the best vehicles for savings

Those skilled in the art of financial planning consider that a sum of between three and six months expenditure constitutes an adequate fund for emergencies. This will depend on your employment status as if you are self-employed then you may need more due to the fact that you will not get sick pay unless you are insured.

This emergency cash should be placed in an account that is readily accessible, probably in an instant access account which allows you to withdraw without penalty. However, these accounts traditionally pay the lowest form of interest and it is advisable to shop around.

There are a number of accounts which offer a higher rate of interest with instant access. You are provided with a card so that you can gain access to your money as and when you need it. If the account is joint then both partners should be provided with a card. Although some of the providers are large established institutions, some are smaller companies with far less capital. You should always think before investing with any company. Think about your needs and requirements and the security of your capital. Which? has a comparison site:

www.moneycompare.which.co.uk/savings-and-isas/instant-access-savings-accounts-that you may find useful.

Cash returns

A lot of savers like to have more cash on deposit than they need for emergencies. If you do not need access to the money for emergencies then it is better to put your money in a higher rate account, one which generally needs notice of withdrawal. The longer the period of notice the more interest that you will get on your money.

Postal accounts pay higher than standard rates of interest and these are useful for those savers who do not require access to their savings over a foreseeable period. One good website which compares rates on postal accounts is:

www.fairinvestment.co.uk/postal_savings_accounts.aspx

You can also get an idea of interest rates by perusing the pages of the dailies and weekend editions of papers, which compare the costs of borrowing and returns on savings. In the United Kingdom rates for deposits are usually quoted gross of tax.

The nominal rate is the rate of interest applied to the account, while the annual effective rate (AER) is the rate taking into account the frequency of interest payments.

The nominal rate is not affected by whether you draw your interest or leave it in the account. But if interest is paid more than once a year and you leave it there, you will earn interest in interest and end the year with more in your account.

If you plan to spend all your interest, you can compare different accounts on the basis of their nominal interest rates. If you plan to leave the interest to accumulate, as the table shows, an account with a lower nominal interest rate could give you a better deal if it is credited more frequently. In this case, you should use the annual effective rate as a comparison.

Personal savings allowances

Since April 2016, savers have been able to grow their money tax free, thanks to the 'personal savings allowance.' This allowance allows you to earn interest up to £1,000 interest tax-free if you're a basic-rate (20%) taxpayer, or £500 if you're a higher-rate (40%) taxpayer. Additional-rate taxpayers don't receive a personal savings allowance, so if you earn more than £150,000 each year, you'll need to pay tax on all your savings.

All interest from savings will be paid gross, which means tax will no longer be deducted by your bank or building society. HMRC has provided a few useful examples to illustrate how the allowance works in practice for basic and higher-rate taxpayers: You earn £20,000 a year and get £250 in account interest – you won't pay any tax because it's less than your £1,000 allowance. You earn £20,000 a year and get £1,500 in account interest – you won't pay tax on your interest up to £1,000. But you'll need to pay basic rate tax (20%) on the £500 above this. You earn £60,000 a year and get £250 in account interest – you won't pay any tax because it's less than your £500 allowance. You earn £60,000 a year and get £1,100 in account interest – you won't pay tax on your interest up to £500. But you'll need to pay higher rate tax (40%) on the £600 above this.

Savings income covered by the personal savings allowance

The personal savings allowance applies to interest you earn from any non-Isa savings accounts and current accounts. There are exceptions – namely Isas and some NS&I savings products, such as Premium bonds. These aren't covered by the personal savings allowance, because they are already tax free. The personal savings allowance applies to some investments, too. You can use your personal savings allowance against interest earned from: government or corporate bonds, peer-to-peer lending interest, interest distributions, i.e. income from bond funds, from authorised unit trusts, open-ended investment companies and investment trusts.

In a nutshell, whether your investment income is taxed as savings or as a dividend depends on the underlying investments. Income from loan-based investments, including the above, will be taxed as interest, while profits from equity investments (buying shares in companies) are taxed as dividend income. Profit from rental properties is taxed in the same way as work or pensions income.

Can interest from savings push me into a higher tax bracket?

Yes, savings income within the allowance still counts towards the basic or higher-rate limits – and may therefore affect the level you're entitled to and the rate of tax due on any excess income. So, if you are a basic-rate taxpayer and you earn enough interest from savings to be pushed into the higher-rate tax threshold, you are only entitled to a £500 allowance and will pay 40% tax on the remainder. In 2020-21, the higher-rate tax threshold in most of the UK is £50,000, the same as in 2019-20. In Scotland, the higher-rate threshold works slightly differently. You pay 41% income tax on income above £43,430 in 2020-21, unchanged from 2019-20.

Exceed personal savings allowance

In most cases, any tax due will be collected automatically through the pay-as-you-earn (PAYE) system, using information provided by banks and building societies. You should be issued with a 'notice of coding' if this is the case. Or, it can be declared on a self-assessment tax return as normal if you usually complete one. Under long-term plans to transform the current tax system, interest could eventually be processed directly from individual digital tax accounts.

Paying too much tax on interest

You can reclaim tax paid on your savings interest, if your bank or building society didn't make use of your full personal savings allowance. Fill in form R40 to claim the tax you were wrongly charged. You can claim tax on savings from up to four tax years ago. It'll normally take around six weeks to get your money back.

The 'savings starter rate'

In addition to the personal savings allowance, an extra tax break already helps those on a low income pay either no tax or reduced tax on their savings. This £5,000 'starting rate for savings' means anyone with total taxable income under their personal income tax allowance plus £5,000 will not pay any tax on your savings. This means if your total taxable income is less than £17,500 for 2020-21, you won't pay any tax on your savings. It helps to think of these allowances sitting on top of each other; first the personal allowance (£12,500 for 2020-

21), then the £5,000 starting savings rate at 0%, and finally the personal savings allowance worth up to £1,000. When HMRC calculates the tax you owe, they'll first look at your income from other sources, and then from your savings income.

So for example, if you earn £14,000 a year from a part-time job and £5,000 interest from savings, this is how you would be taxed in 2020-21: 0% on the first £12,500 income from your job = £0 20% tax on the remaining £1,500 from your wages (£14,000 less the £12,500 personal income tax allowance) = £300 0% tax on £3,500 of your savings (because you've lost £1,500 of the 0% savings band from your earnings over the personal allowance) = £0 0% tax on the remaining £1,000 of your savings using your £1,000 personal savings allowance = £0 20% tax on the remaining £500 savings interest = £100 Total tax bill = £400.

Are ISA's worth it?

Even though there are now generous tax breaks on savings, and interest on non-Isa savings accounts tends to be higher, there are still significant long-term benefits to Isas, particularly if you're a high earner or you have substantial savings. It's likely that the best way to boost returns and minimise tax is to combine a range of savings products and Isas, as well as high-interest current accounts if you don't mind switching banks. It's also worth bearing in mind that the personal savings allowance will protect your interest from tax this year – but if you're growing savings over the long term once they're in your Isa they'll be tax free forever. Read below about various scams relating to ISA's

*

The choice of accounts

There are a wide variety of accounts available from banks and building societies. Many accounts have differing features. Most pay variable interest but some pay fixed rates. The following are some of the accounts on offer.

Children's accounts

These accounts sometimes offer better variable rates than can be gained on a small deposit on a regular savings account. These accounts can also offer free gifts for children, such as magazines, moneyboxes etc.

A good website which will give you an idea of the entire range of savings accounts available to children, such as Child trust Funds, Junior ISA's etc is www.deal-review.co.uk. Another useful site is www.moneysavingexpert.com

Instant access accounts

These permit withdrawal of capital without notice, though there is usually a restriction on how much cash can be withdrawn on one day. The interest rate is variable. Interest may be credited yearly, half yearly, quarterly, monthly or daily. With most accounts, the rate will depend on the amount invested. You can get a good idea of the various savings accounts by accessing the numerous comparison sites or by looking at the weekend papers, such as the Times, Telegraph, Guardian etc.

Individual Savings Accounts (ISA's)

There are numerous ISA's on the market. The mainstream ISA allows you to invest up to £20,000 per annum in either a cash ISA or a stocks and shares ISA or a mixture of the two. In addition, there is a new lifetime ISA (LISA), launched from

April 2017, which can be taken out by those between 18-40 and which is designed to help people to save for the longer term, and can help to boost pension savings. Up to £4,000 per year can be saved in a LISA and the state will boost this with an annual bonus of 25%. the bonus is paid until you hit 50. The bonus is paid annually in the 2020/2021 tax year and then monthly in the following tax years. The bonus is paid on contributions and the maximum bonus you can get is £32,000.

One very good site for ISA rates is www.top-isa-rates.co.uk.

Children's ISA's (JISA) have a savings limit of £9,000 from April 2020/21. They remain tax-fee up until 18yrs old and can provide good vehicles to build up a lump sum for the future. www.moneysavingexpert.com/savings/junior-isa is a good site to explore for information regarding children's ISA's. In addition, there are numerous other sites.

Savings APPS and other savings devices for children
The saving apps that give parents a helping hand

Financial technology companies are offering a range of innovative and easy ways to save for children

A couple, both 35, want their 17-month-old daughter to have a nest egg when she turns 18, but it is easy to forget to put money aside every month. The family use a new investing app called Beanstalk, which rounds up their everyday spending and invests the leftover money on their daughters behalf in a Junior Isa. She will be able to get the money when she turns 18 and spend it how she likes.

The couple say that they save £50 a month by allowing Beanstalk to travel through their bank account to see where it can round up recent purchases to the nearest £10. They are also aiming to save £200 a month from their own income. Beanstalk is only available for parents to use, rather than the children, but the company is working on a version for children so they can see their investments grow. Grandparents can contribute and see how much they have paid into their grandchild's Isa, but will not be able to see the total amount in the fund. Beanstalk charges a 0.5 per cent fee for any money invested via the app, without any exit or setup charges. Parents pay fees of 0.12 to 0.15 per cent for the money to be invested in an exchange-traded fund, also known as a tracker, so called because they follow shares in a particular market index.

There are two funds to choose from, a lower-risk Legal & General Cash Trust fund and a higher-risk Fidelity Index World fund, which tracks the MSCI global share market. Parents can allocate all or some of their money to each one in 10 per cent increments.

As with the rules around Junior Isas, it is possible to save up to £9,000 a year for each child. Another option is to take out a traditional cash Junior Isa and drip-feed the money into the child's account. These benefits from higher than average cash savings rates. The top-paying cash Junior Isa, from National Savings & Investments (NS&I) pays 3.25 per cent and can be opened online from £1 (however check this as rates are changing all the time). The next best rate is from Coventry Building Society, at 2.95 per cent, which can be opened by phone or post or in branches. In contrast, the best adult Isa, from Cynergy Bank, pays just 0.9 per cent. If parents want their child to be more involved with saving their pocket money, they can use a dedicated app. Go Henry, for six to 18-year-olds, comes with a prepaid debit card and can be accessed by the parents and child. The parent can control when their child gets pocket money, such as after they have done a particular household chore.

Parents can also control whether the child can use the card for online transactions, with certain sites such as gambling companies always blocked. Go Henry costs £2,99 a month for each child. Another app. Osper, has a prepaid debit card that parents can top up using the app and add regular pocket money payments to. It's also possible to lock and unlock the linked card.

The app costs £2.50 a month for each child, with an additional 50p fee for when friends and family want to top up the card. Nimbi is an app and prepaid Master-card debit card for children aged 8-18, where parents can monitor their spending and top it up in the app.

A round-up feature similar to Beanstalk means that children can transfer their spare pennies from transactions into a savings account. Children do not earn interest on the savings.

Parents can also disable cash withdrawals from the card and remotely unlock the card, which costs £15 a year. Rooster Money, which has a basic free version, helps children budget and save by showing them a virtual star and reward chart and money tracker.

The basic version without a card aims to help children save. The £24.99-a-year prepaid card version comes with parental controls.

A note of caution generally with ISA's
Watch out – Online scammers

The internet is awash with bogus Isa providers trying to persuade you to part with your cash – and the run-up to the end of the tax year is likely to be a time when scammers ramp up their efforts.

Dozens of scam websites are offering eye-catching rates, sometimes touting returns in double figures, and they often appear at the top of Google searches for terms such as "top Isa rates" and "protected savings" .The also use words such as "secure", "safe" and "low-risk" to convince savers their money will be protected. Some use logos of official bodies that do not back them, as well as falsely claiming association with reputable organisations such as Trustpilot and national newspapers.

The Sunday Times and campaigners have reported more than 100 suspicious-looking websites to the City regulator, the Financial Conduct Authority (FCA). Many have paid Google for prominence and appear with an "Ad" logo next to them. Although Google will eliminate a scam website from its search results when informed, many change their names or internet address and then reappear. Google says that it has robust systems in place to monitor scam sites and remove companies that do not comply with its rules. The FCA and big insurers have called for tougher legislation to force Google to take them down.

The government says that the FCA already has strong powers to tackle the problem. While scammers can continue taking advantage of laws to advertise their schemes, it is important to be on your guard against bogus deals.

How to spot a scam Isa site

Scam websites will typically advertise rates that are much higher than those available on the high street or via well known comparison websites such as Moneyfacts and Moneysupermarket. For example, some have offered annual returns as high as 30 per cent. The most you can hope to get from a well-known brand is about 2per cent. The websites may also deliberately conflate different types of Isa: for example, regular Isas and innovative finance Isas. The latter invest in loans and are not protected by the Financial Services Compensation Scheme (FSCS), the government safety net to protect savers in case anything goes wrong. Most will not have a company number, address or telephone contact number. No respectable organisation offering financial services would leave out such details. Instead, savers are invited to enter an email address or telephone number, after which they will receive emails from high-risk or fraudulent firms. The websites effectively act as unregulated introducers to these dodgy providers. Should you be contacted, the caller may say they can offer you a rare opportunity to save in something that has guaranteed returns. They may also tell you there is only a narrow window of opportunity, to pressure you into investing. Never be Pressured. You may be sent authentic-looking documents by email that will, without permission, use the branding of well-known firms such as Axa, Blackrock or Barclays. Do not be taken in. Some of the websites will provide an address in a high-end postcode. This will also often claim to be protected by the FSCS. Use its website to check, fscs.org.uk If you see a great deal, check the FCA's fraud warning list to see if the watchdog believes that it is a scam, and do some research to confirm that a company has the professional backing it claims to have. You can check the FCA's register to see if a firm is authorised. If it is, use the contact details that the company gives you, to avoid being duped by fraudulent "clone" of a genuine organisation. Many promotions appear to break rules stating that only regulated financial firms can promote investments – an offence punishable by up to two years in prison.

Monthly income accounts

These types of accounts may have a minimum notice period for withdrawal. The income is usually paid direct to your current account and there is usually a £250 minimum amount. www.thisismoney.co.uk shows a good range of monthly income accounts.

Notice accounts

Money can be withdrawn without penalty by giving the appropriate amount of notice. If you withdraw without notice you will lose interest on the amount you would have been paid during the notice period. There is usually a minimum deposit of £1000 or more. there are numerous websites giving details of notice accounts and also the weekend supplements in the main newspapers also provide information.

Time deposits

The interest rate is fixed for the time of the deposit, often 30 days onwards. There will be a penalty for early withdrawal. Interest is usually added at the end of the period that is fixed and is usually gross of tax.

Fixed-rate investments

You can commit your money for a fixed period; say five years, at a certain rate of interest, say 3%. If rates are at 0.5% this may seem attractive but rates can rise during the period. Before investing for the longer term at fixed rates you should consider carefully the market in the longer term and decide whether you want to make this gamble. Fixed interest rates will offer you a reasonable return over the period and it is difficult to predict interest rates over the longer term. Again, the main websites, such as this ismoney will provide comparisons, as will the financial pages of the main newspapers.

Short-term fixed-rate investments-Escalator bonds

These are issued by building societies and pay a rate of interest that rises each year for a fixed period. Since these are fixed rate accounts you cannot get it back early or there can be a significant financial penalty.

You should always think about the consequences of your wish to invest in this type of product.

Fixed rate bonds

These accounts pay a flat fixed rate of interest for a fixed period from one to five years. Early withdrawal is not usually permitted without a penalty. There be a minimum investment.

Guaranteed growth bonds

Issued by insurance companies, these guarantee a fixed rate for a specified period, usually between two and five years. A lump sum is paid at the end of the term. The return is treated as having borne basic rate tax so there will only be an additional liability if you are a higher rate taxpayer.

Guaranteed income bonds

These pay a fixed income for a specified term, usually two to five years. The tax treatment is the same as for the above bonds.

National Savings Certificates

These grow in value at a fixed rate for a period of up to five years. The profits are exempt from tax and there are limits on how much you can invest.

National Savings Pensioners Guaranteed Bonds

These pay a fixed amount of income over two to five years. The interest is taxable but is paid without deduction at source.

Unit trust savings plans

Unit trusts and open-ended investment companies are similar in having a pool of money which they manage on behalf of individual and corporate investors. The pool expands or contracts depending on the additions or withdrawals into it and the value of a unit or share is the value of the investments in the pool divided by the number of units or shares in issue. A wide variety of funds are available, investing in a variety of areas and countries. Minimum monthly savings are from £30-£50. The income received is taxable and will usually be taxed at source. Higher rate taxpayers will receive a certificate showing what they have paid at source and they will be personally responsible for any extra payments. Costs vary from 1%-5% of each contribution with an annual charge of

0.5% to 2% of the value of your assets. You can take out a plan in the name of a child.

Investment trusts

Unlike unit trusts or open-ended investment companies, investment trusts do not issue new shares to savers but buy existing shares through the stock market. This is because investment trusts have a fixed pool of assets and the price of a share in the market may be higher or lower than its net asset value. These schemes are run by investment trust managers. They usually subsidise the costs of the plan, which are much lower than the costs of buying investment trust shares through a stockbroker. The annual charges are between 0.5% and 2%. The taxation rules and child rules are the same as for unit trusts.

With profits savings plans

With profits savings plans are in the form of endowment polices issued by insurance companies. Though they are life policies, they provide very little life cover. Most of the premiums that are paid are used to invest in the companies with profits fund, which is a giant pool of assets usually worth billions of pounds. The fund will hold a variety of assets including fixed rate investments, UK and overseas shares and property.

The with-profits policy has a sum assured, which is the minimum amount that is paid on death or at the maturity rate. Two types of bonus are added to the sum assured. Reversionary bonuses are added each year, often at quite a lower rate of 3% or so. At maturity (or death) a terminal bonus is added which can be equal to al the reversionary bonuses paid. Once a reversionary bonus has been added to a policy, it cannot be taken away, but terminal bonus rates are not guaranteed and can be varied at any time. With-profits policies are of two types. Some have one fixed maturity date, while with a 'flexible policy' you can en-cash it at several different dates, usually at five-year intervals. The charges for with profits policies are typically about 12-15% of premiums over the term. The term for these policies is usually quite long, being anything from 10-25 years so careful thought needs to be given to this type of investment. They are only really suitable if you can sustain your savings over this long period.

Friendly society plans

Friendly societies are permitted to run tax-free savings schemes with low minimum and maximum investments. Some are of the with-profit types, while others are unit-linked. The plans have a minimum term of ten years and the high costs can wipe out other benefits so again careful thought has to be given to this type of investment.

The purpose of saving

The purposes of saving, as we have seen, are many and will differ, depending on your circumstances and long-term view. Some of the more usual savings objectives are to provide retirement income, to pay for children's education (see later) to reduce debt such as mortgage and for general purposes, for life's little luxuries. Whatever you choose you should do so carefully, think about the short and long-term advantages and don't take unnecessary risks.

Other savings schemes-peer-to-peer lending

Peer to peer lending is for those who wish to take a gamble

with their savings in order to obtain a better rate of return than that offered by mainstream banks.

What is peer-to-peer?

Peer-to-peer lending enables individuals to lend to each other, bypassing the need for a traditional bank or building society. Money from individual lenders is put together to fund borrowers seeking personal or small business loans and in some cases, buy-to-let mortgages. Lending in the sector reached 6billion by the end of June 2017, according to the peer-to-peer finance association. Platforms such as Zoopla and Ratesetter display rates based on how long your money is locked up for and how risky a borrower is deemed to be by the platform.

As with the savings market, the longer your money is tied up for the better the rate of return. The products work like a normal savings product, paying interest monthly or quarterly but accessing your funds can be more difficult because the process relies on another lender wanting to buy and there may be an access fee. You can earn your interest tax free using the Innovative Tax-Free ISA. At the time of writing many platforms are waiting approval from the Financial Conduct Authority for ISA manager status.

Peer-to-peer loans do not benefit from the Financial Services Compensation Scheme, which protects up to £85,000 of savings, but if you invest via a financial advisor you benefit from £85,000 protection.

Investing a Lump Sum

If you are able to consider investing a lump sum of money, you must take great care in establishing your requirements for that investment and also your own future plans.

For example:

- you may not be worried about getting a significant return as long as it is likely to better the return you would get from your building society account;
- you need the best return possible over the next five years without jeopardizing capital;
- you aren't worried how the money is invested provided you don't receive a tax bill;

Quite clearly, the important issues to remember when investing a lump sum are:

1. the amount of money you can afford to invest;
2. the term of the investment;
3. the risk involved with the investment;
4. tax implications.

As we have already seen, there are numerous ways in which you can invest your money and the same considerations should be made whether you are saving on a regular basis or a lump sum.

The options available

Your choice of investment will obviously depend on your own personal financial circumstances. Below you will find details of the most popular investments currently available.

Higher interest building society accounts

If you are concerned about the risk attached with investing your money, then you cannot do a lot better than your building society. Although some people may consider investing in their building society as unattractive, with rates now at the time of writing at an all time low, you haven't got any worries about how your money is being invested. For lump sums, building societies often offer a wide range of higher rate accounts with a tiered rate of interest, depending on the size of investment. Most higher rate accounts have a notice period which must be given for any withdrawals. This may not apply, however, if the balance of the account remains over £5,000. A large number of higher rate accounts will allow you to take a regular income on a monthly basis. Remember, from April 2016, the first £1000 of interest received from savings is tax fee. A good site comparing building society accounts is www.money.co.uk/savings-accounts.htm

Ordinary accounts

This is a basic account which will allow you to invest between £10-£10,000.

Index linked Savings certificates

This is a good way of investing your money over a five-year period especially if interest rates are high. The interest you will receive is fixed and tax-free. For more details about this type of investment go to www.nsandi.com.

Investment bonds

Investment bonds are considered a medium to long-term investment and the investment options range from the with profits investments to investments in the property markets and overseas. The risk is always a major factor in any investment and you should be aware exactly where your money is being invested and the relative risk.

All major insurance companies offer investment bonds and they can be used for both capital growth and income if required. The investment fund is taxable and payments are made net of basic rate tax. There is an allowance however, which will allow both basic rate and higher rate taxpayers to withdraw up to 5% of the fund value each year without liability.

The minimum amount that you can invest in a bond is normally £2,000 and you should consider investing it for a minimum of five years. In the case of an emergency, you would be able to gain access to your money but the value will relate to the period of investment, charges and market conditions.

The main points to remember are that you should invest in a bond that suits your attitude to risk. If you are a higher rate taxpayer you may be able to reduce any liability if you can cash in the bond when the income drops to the basic rate bracket.

Guaranteed Capital Investments

This is a relatively new concept in the insurance industry as your investment is directly linked to the performance of the FTSE one hundred. If you read the financial press or watch the main television news you will always see a reference to the FTSE one hundred. It provides a clear indication of how the stock market is behaving as it monitors the share prices of the top 100 companies in the UK.

From day to day the prices of each company's shares can change for any reason and towards the bottom of the index the smaller companies are constantly competing to secure their position within the top 100.

The growth of the FTSE is often compared to that of banks

and building societies (see single premium investments) and over a long term period is considered to be a valuable alternative to the standard options. Traditionally, the FTSE has outperformed the returns offered by building society accounts and for that reason most insurance companies will guarantee that on completion of the five year term you will at least receive your original investment, thereby reducing the risk factor.

The minimum investment is usually £6,000 and the fund and benefits are paid net of basic rate tax. Guaranteed capital investments are offered on limited availability and are not able to provide an income. They are, however, a worthwhile consideration when you are building up an investment portfolio..

A good website here is www.bestinvestor.co.uk/Guaranteed_Capital_Funds although at the time of writing (October 2020) the website is undergoing a refreshment. there are numerous other websites, such as Hargreaves Lansdowne https://www.hl.co.uk/Buy-Funds/Online

Unit Trusts

The purpose of the unit trust is to give individuals the opportunity to invest directly in the stock market. There are a multitude of investment opportunities ranging from UK equities to shares in Japan and North America. In order to overcome the charges and realise a profit, you must look at investing your money in a unit trust for at least three years or longer.

Unit trusts can be used for capital growth or income and you should obtain help from a financial advisor to choose the most suitable trust for your performance. Once you have chosen your trust and paid your money, you will be issued with a certificate. It is very important that you keep this in a safe place as you will need to produce it when you cash it in.

To establish how well your investment is doing, you can phone the trust managers or look at the share page of any quality newspaper. You will normally see two columns, the offer price and the bid price. For the purpose of selling you must multiply the bid price by the number of units you hold. A good site for more information about unit trusts is www.money.co.uk

The tax implications

Unless you are a higher rate tax-payer it is unlikely that you will have any tax liability on the income or gain of the investment. If you are a higher rate tax-payer there are various ways of mitigating your liability and you should discuss this with a financial advisor before committing yourself to any investment.

A quick word about crypto currencies

Since the last edition of this book, cryptocurrencies such as bitcoin have come to the fore. quite a few people in the know have invested in them However, it is the case that most people don't understand them and wouldn't go near them. Not surpising, as there are an awful lot of scams out there. Below is a brief outline of crypto-currencies.

What is a cryptocurrency?

Bitcoin was the first cryptocurrency, and is still the biggest, but in the eight years since it was created pretenders to the throne have come along.

All of them have the same basic underpinnings: they use a

"blockchain", a shared public record of transactions, to create and track a new type of digital token – one that can only be made and shared according to the agreed-upon rules of the network, whatever they may be.some cryptocurrencies, such as Litecoin or Dogecoin, fulfil the same purpose as bitcoin – building a new digital currency – with tweaks to some of the details (making transactions faster, for instance, or ensuring a basic level of inflation). Others, such as Ethereum or Bat, take the same principle but apply it to a specific purpose: cloud computing or digital advertising in the case of those two.

What exactly is a bitcoin? Can I hold one?

A bitcoin doesn't really exist as a concrete physical – or even digital – object. If I have 0.5 bitcoins sitting in my digital wallet, that doesn't mean there is a corresponding other half sitting somewhere else.

What you really have when you own a bitcoin is the collective agreement of every other computer on the bitcoin network that your bitcoin was legitimately created by a bitcoin "miner", and then passed on to you through a series of legitimate transactions.

If you want to actually own some bitcoin, there are two options: either become a miner (which involves investing a lot of money in computers and electricity bills – probably more than the value of the bitcoin you'll actually make, unless you're very smart), or simply buy some bitcoin from someone else using conventional money, typically through a bitcoin exchange such as Coinbase or Bitfinex.

What can I actually do with cryptocurrencies?

Bitcoin can be used as a payment system for a few online transactions, and even fewer real-world ones.

As I stated above, although it is good to understand what all the fuss is about, investing in bitcoin and other cryptocurrencies is not for the fain hearted and I would not recommend it unless you have a firm grasp of the nature of the beast! There are numerous websites recommending that you invest in bitcoin, avoid them unless you are sure of what you are doing.

Savings APPS

Automated savings plans are offered by money apps that use algorithms to analyse your spending habits. Savings apps such as Chips, Tandem, Moneybox and Plum work out how much money you can afford to squirrel away – and make the transfer on your behalf. Plum analyses your daily spend and transfers small amounts into a savings account about five times a month. You can choose between six settings to guide the app on how much to save. It is a good way to get into savings habit, although some app accounts do not pay the best interest rates. Plum's easy access account, for example, pays just 0.6 per cent. Some pay nothing at all. You can authorise the robots behind some of the apps to round up the spare change from your debits card transactions and stash away the difference. For instance, if your coffee costs £2.00, 80p is automatically transferred to a nominated savings account. Some of the high street banks are on board too, Lloyds Banking Group (Lloyds, Halifax and Bank of Scotland) offers a similar Save the Change service. Nationwide customers can do the same using its Impulse Saver. If it is better rates you are looking for, the cash savings platform Octopus Cash, Raisin, Flagstone and Hargreaves Lansdown Active Savings give you automatic access to a range of accounts with banks. Once registered with Octopus Cash, for example, you can switch between seven partner banks, which means you do not need to spend time filling in forms to open an account with a new company; You can do it with a few clicks online. These platforms are typically for large cash savings.

**

Ch. 5

Protecting Your Income

_____

We all realise the importance of life insurance and the main lesson has been to check the policy thoroughly before buying. We do however mainly neglect the need to ensure that there is adequate protection to cover accidents or illness that prevent us from working and therefore maintaining our normal standard of living.   Most employers restrict the length of time that they will make full payment to the employee in the event of illness and the self employed are likely to receive even less.

What is income protection insurance?

Formerly known as permanent health insurance (PHI), long-term income protection (IP) is an insurance policy that pays out if you're unable to work because of injury or illness. IP usually pays out until retirement, death or your return to work, although Short Term IP (Stip) policies are also available at a lower cost. Neither IP or Stip pays out if you're made redundant - but they will often provide 'back to work' help if you're off sick.

Is income protection the same as PPI?

Income protection isn't the same as the widely miss-sold payment protection insurance (PPI). Where PPI covers a particular debt and any payouts go to your lender, income protection hands you a tax-free proportion of your income if you're unable to work because of illness or injury. How you spend the money is up to you.

Why do I need IP?

Only a minority of employers support their staff for more than a year if they're off sick from work. Given the low level of state benefits available, everyone of working age should consider IP.

Millions of us have policies such as private medical insurance and payment protection insurance, sold to us over the years by salespeople who convinced us we needed protecting. However, while they were right about the protection, they were often wrong about the policies. The one protection policy every working adult in the UK should consider is the very one most of us don't have - income protection.

How much will IP cost?

Your health, whether you smoke and level of cover needed will weigh into your premium, but your type of job also plays a major part in determining what you'll pay. Many insurers group jobs into four categories of risk, though some have more. For example, jobs may be divided into the following groups:

Class 1: Professional; managers; administrative staff; staff with limited business mileage; admin clerk; computer programmer; secretary.

Class 2: Some workers with high business mileage; skilled manual work; engineer; florist; shop assistant

Class 3: Skilled manual workers and some semi-skilled workers; care worker; plumber; teacher

Class 4: Heavy manual workers and some unskilled workers; bar person; construction worker; mechanic

How much does income protection pay out?

Income protection payouts are usually based on a percentage of your earnings: 50% to 70% is the norm. Payments are tax-free. IP policies pay out only once a pre-agreed period has passed, generally ranging from one to 12 months after you put in a claim. The longer the 'deferral' period you choose, the lower your premiums. The default deferral period tends to be 13 or 26 weeks.

Most IP providers report paying high proportions of claims made to them. For 2015, insurance giant Aviva published that it had paid 92.4% of IP claims, while LV paid 92%. British Friendly paid out 96.7%.

What about ASU?

ASU (Accident, Sickness and Unemployment Cover? policies are a cheaper alternative, named because - depending on your choice - you can buy policies to cover you in the event of accident, sickness or unemployment. Like Stip policies, they'll typically provide cover for around one to two years. The main difference with ASU policies is they're sold without full medical underwriting - which means you have less certainty that you'll be covered when you put in a claim.

Cover offered by banks and building societies

The threat of losing your job is common in today's society and it is something that could ruin your lifestyle and bring great hardship to you and your family.

The banks and building societies are of course aware of this and therefore offer you the opportunity to apply for a scheme which will protect you and your partner (in the case of a joint mortgage) against accident or sickness or involuntary redundancy. This is sometimes referred to as mortgage payment protection or payment care.

The premiums for these types of schemes range from £6 per £100 of cover to £9 per £100. A claim can only be made and benefits paid once you have been unable to work for a period of three months, after which stage the benefits are normally paid for a period of one to two years for sickness and also for redundancy. Some insurers when paying benefit will send a cheque direct to your lender each month to ensure you are using the money for the purpose that was intended.

These schemes have proved very popular and you should seek further information about them from the relevant lender, as you are not likely to be given a chance to take out a policy after your mortgage has been completed.

You can also allow for extra benefit from these policies to cover the cost of any endowments or life insurances that may run in conjunction with the mortgage.

This type of cover is of benefit to the employed but the redundancy cover is obviously of no benefit to the self-employed and a good permanent health insurance would be more relevant. If the benefits of the scheme are paid direct to you, that would constitute income and income tax would be payable at the relevant rate.

**

Ch. 6

Borrowing Money

At this point in time, particularly because of the effects of the pandemic, we are borrowing more and more money. Indeed, if we look at the papers we can see that we are a 'nation in debt'. However, if you can possibly avoid credit, it is much better to do so. When you buy goods on credit or you borrow money you are, in most cases, taking out a high interest loan. It is the aim of banks to sell money for the highest rate possible in order to make profits. The best bet, at the end of the day, is the consumer. Better than the stock market or any other investment.

Obviously, in some cases you will need to borrow money. The main point is that if you do have to borrow get the best deal possible. Read the small print. It is really surprising how few people shop around for a good deal and end up paying over the odds.

Caution before you borrow

One question that you need to ask yourself before you borrow is: do I really need to borrow? Many people are tempted to borrow money even when they have money saved. This is mainly because it is a nice feeling having money in the bank. However, this is an illusion. The interest you pay on your borrowings will always be more than the savings. To borrow when you have enough in the bank to pay for an item is false economy.

If you do not have savings, you should think very carefully

about whether you really need to spend the money now or whether you can wait. If borrowing is absolutely necessary it is important to know what repayments you can afford. The quicker you can clear a loan the less you will pay. Once you have run up credit, make repaying it a priority.

Comparisons of costs

It is a fact that any lender will be happy to give you credit, providing that you are seen as creditworthy. If you are in the process of getting a loan make sure that you have shopped around, including using the Internet. To find the cheapest credit you will need to compare different lenders interest rates in the form of their APR (Annual Percentage Rate).

The APR is designed to show the true cost of borrowing, and all lenders must calculate it the same way. Arrangement fees and any other charges must be included in the calculation as well as interests. How and when payments are made is also taken into account. This allows you to make direct comparisons between different forms of borrowing, so check that you are being quoted the APR and not the monthly rate of interest which sounds a lot less but is usually more.

Generally, the lower the APR. the lower the cost of credit, but make sure that the deals that you compare are for the same repayment period. The APR, as the name implies, is the cost of credit over one year at a time. If you spread the repayment of a loan over two years the cost will be more than one year even if the APR is lower.

The APR may not be the only factor to take into account when comparing loans. Some lenders will reduce the APR if you take out protection insurance, usually making the overall package more expensive. You should also consider whether rates are fixed or variable. Fixed rates protect you from rate rises and enable you to budget but your payments won't fall either. If rates are reduced your payments are fixed and will not reduce.

This is very much a calculation that you have to make. In today's low interest rate climate it may be that any further reduction may be so negligible as not to affect your judgment.

Payment protection insurance

Payment protection insurance is usually offered with credit nowadays. However, bearing in mind the recent huge problems with PPI, and the agreement by the banks to compensate those policyholders who were miss-sold insurance, this again is down to your own judgment. Without a doubt this insurance is useful if you are unemployed or have an accident and cannot pay the loans.

CHECK THE POLICY BEFORE YOU COMMIT!.

Borrowing to pay off other loans

We are bombarded with moneylenders, or their agents (companies set up to sell money on behalf of others) who tell us how prudent it is to put all your eggs in one basket. This normally involves re-mortgaging. You should try to restrict yourself to conventional lenders. In many cases, it will appear cheaper in the short-term to borrow money over a long period. You will save on the monthly outgoings but pay a lot more over the period of the loan. If you need to go down this route you will probably find that re-mortgaging with a bank or building society will be a lot cheaper than a secured loan.

Overdrafts

If you want to borrow for a short period an authorised

overdraft will be a good option, providing that your bank offers competitive terms. Some banks charge arrangement fees for borrowing, others will apply relatively high rates. Many will have a combination of both. If you overdraw without permission, which the banks favour, the interest rates charged will double. The advantages of overdrafts are that they are flexible but the amounts that you can borrow are limited.

Credit cards

Credit cards are one of the easiest and most popular ways of borrowing money. They are convenient and flexible and there is no need to approach the lender other than in the first instance when applying for a card. Maximum limits vary depending on your own circumstances, but can be between £1000 and £15000 (usually). The balance that you run up on your card can be paid as quickly or slowly as you wish subject to a monthly limit, usually 3% or £5 whichever is the lower.

If you clear your monthly balance in full there will be no interest charge. This means that you can gain up to 59 days interest free credit between the time that the transaction took place and the time that it takes you to pay the bill. If you do not pay the balance in full then interest is charged.

Interest rates on credit cards vary greatly. They can range between 5-20% and more, depending on the deal on offer. Many card companies try to attract customers by offering reduced rates on balance transfers. Some give these low introductory rates on new purchases as well. The introductory rate usually lasts six months. This can be useful if you want to spread the payments over a few months but contain the interest payment. Buying goods and services by credit card can make sense in other ways. If you use your card to buy something worth between £100 and £30,000 you will normally qualify for extra protection under section 75 of the Consumer Credit Act, which makes the card issuer jointly liable with the supplier if there is a problem with the goods. Other perks can also be offered by the card supplier such as free travel insurance.

Add your debt to your Netflix, gym and veg box subscription

A new service offers to lend you money for a fixed fee over 12-month contract. It's simple, but is it value for money.

A subscription company marketing itself as the "loan facility for smart people" comes with an annual interest rate more expensive than any mainstream credit card. Creditspring has lent £3 million to almost 8, 000 customers since it opened in September 2018. It charges £6 a month membership for two £250 loans, or £8 a month for two £500 loans. Borrowers have to pay back loans before taking out the other and sign a contract to pay the charges every month for a year, even if they pay the loan back early. Two loans of £250 over 12 months would cost £72. This makes an annual percentage rate (APR) of 87.4 per cent. APR is the measure used for comparing the costs of credit cards and other borrowing. It does not give an idea of the actual amount you will pay, but is useful for comparison purposes on loans with the same repayment period (see box).

The highest APR for a mainstream credit card is 76 per cent from American Express. The average credit card APR, according to Moneyfacts, a financial analysis company, is 22.8 per cent. If you took out two £500 loans with Creditspring over 12 months with an £8 fee, you would have to pay back a total of £1,096 – an APR of 38.6 per cent. Were someone to hold debit of £500 or £1,000 on a credit card with an APR of 39.9 per cent, and pay it off over a year (with one month interest free), they would pay £30 less in the first scenario and £15 less in the second.

Why APR is not that helpful

Lenders are obliged to quote an annual percentage rate (APR) when they set out costs of a loan or credit card, but this is not always a helpful equation. An APR takes compound interest and other costs into account, and is based on the assumption that a loan will be paid off within 365 days and that the initial monthly cost will be replicated and compounded over a year, which is rarely the case. It is, however, useful as a comparison tool for credit cards.

Because of the (really very complicated) calculation, APR will be a lot more expensive than a flat interest rate but it does not represent the amount you actually pay. If you pay a flat charge on your borrowing every month there will be no compound interest, but the APR calculation assumes that there is. That's why the Creditspring loan has an APR of 87.4 per cent, while in reality what you repay on two £250 loans over a year is actually about 14 per cent of what you borrowed.

Personal loans

Personal loans are offered by many organisations nowadays, with the large supermarkets and insurance companies getting in on the act. These lenders can usually offer competitive rates. So can lenders over the internet. If you want to make a major purchase the vendor will usually offer to arrange a loan but it may be more competitive to seek a personal loan elsewhere.

Personal loans are a useful way of borrowing over the medium term if you cannot get an overdraft to cover the period. Between £5000 and £25000 can normally be obtained over periods of 1-25 years. The more you borrow the lower the APR. You should always carefully scrutinise the rates on offer and don't be misled. If you need a borrowing facility that you can re-use, rather than a one-off sum, some lenders offer flexible loans where you agree a monthly payment and are allowed to borrow a maximum multiple of that amount at any time.

Payday loans

Consumers unable to access credit through traditional banking means are increasingly turning to alternative sources, including payday loan companies. Payday, or paycheque loans, are short-term loans that you get in return for your pay cheque or proof of your income. They are basically cash advances on the salary you are expecting and are available online and on the high street.

They can be a way of getting your hands on your wages quicker than you otherwise would, but it is important to be aware of the high interest rates charged and the consequences of falling behind with your repayment.

This type of borrowing is not suitable for those looking to repay their loans over a long period, as they are designed to be short-term loans to deal with short-term personal cash flow issues. If loans are rolled over, debts could escalate and consumers could get into difficulties. They should only be considered if consumers are confident that they'll be able to repay the debt in full when it is due. If you are considering using a payday loan company, you should look into all the available alternatives first: Speak to your bank manager as you may be able to get an agreed overdraft

Look into Social Fund Loans - these are government-funded, interest-free loans available to those on low incomes (see below).

Changes to payday loan regulation

On 1st April, 2014, the FCA (Financial Conduct Authority) took over regulation of the consumer credit market from the OFT (Office of Fair Trading). One of the first things the FCA did was to crack down on lenders that offer 'High Cost Short Term Credit' (HCSTC), and this includes payday loans. The key changes include limiting the number of times a loan can be rolled over.

Currently if you can't afford to repay your payday loan on time you can usually roll it over to the next month. This flexibility comes as a cost and can quickly lead to a small short term loan turning into a hefty loan term debt.

Usually the balance of your loan is extended by a month, with extra interest and roll over fees whacked on to your borrowing. You generally only have to pay the interest charges upfront when you roll over a loan - but sometimes this can be rolled over as well.

Under the new FCA rules you will only be able to roll over your loan twice before the balance will be due. This protects you from spiralling debts, while still maintaining some flexibility should you need to extend a loan due to exceptional circumstances. Notably the FCA have chosen to go further than the voluntary Good Practice Charter introduced in 2012, which sets a limit of rollovers to 3.

Stopping lenders from trying to collect payment more than twice

Most payday lenders will use a CPA (Continuous Payment Authority) to collect payment. This is a way of taking money from your bank account that gives the lender the right to take payment on any date they like, and any amount they like. This is important because although lenders should let you know when they plan to take payment and how much it'll be, not all do.

CPAs can be a quick and flexible way to pay your bills as they help you avoid default and late payment charges if the lender tries to collect payment from your account and the money isn't there. However, there is growing concern that they are open to misuse, leading to payday lenders taking money from their customers' accounts without warning.

This causes problems if money is taken ahead of other bills, causing defaults on more important debts like your council tax, utilities, mortgage or rent; and leading to bank charges and future credit issues. Under the new FCA rules, lenders will be limited to only two failed CPA attempts. This means that they can't continually try to withdraw money from your account when you don't have the funds available, and instead will need to contact you to find out what's going on.

This limit can be reset if you decide to refinance or roll over your loan and pay the amount you currently owe.

Banning part payments by CPA

As well as introducing a limit on the number of times lenders can try to collect payment via CPA, they'll also be limited to how much they're able to collect. In addition, caps were introduced from 2nd January 2015 which limits the amount of interest that can be charged. They are as follows:

- Initial cap of 0.8% a day in interest charges. Someone who takes out a loan of £100 over 30 days, and pays back on time, will therefore pay no more than £24 in interest
- A cap of £15 on the one-off default fee. Borrowers who fail to pay back on time can be charged a maximum of £15, plus a maximum of 0.8% a day in interest and fees
- Total cost cap of 100%. If a borrower defaults, the interest on the debt will build up, but he or she will never have to pay back more than twice the amount they borrowed.

Secured or unsecured loans

Most personal loans are unsecured. This means that if you do not pay, the lender can take you to court but does not have the right to seize any property or possessions. With a secured loan assets such as property (usually property) are used, as security and the lender will take a second charge on your property for the value of the loan. This is known as a second charge loan. Nowadays, there is little advantage in taking out a secured loan as you may be able to find a better rate for unsecured loans, unless you have a poor credit rating.

Interest free or low start credit

This type of credit often seems too good to be true. Many people take it up, particularly on cars or furniture. However, nothing is free and you should look carefully at the terms and conditions. You could find that you are signing up to an interest-bearing loan, with interest waived only if you pay up in full during an initial period. If you miss the deadline to pay of the balance then hefty interest charges will be incurred. The main principle is that you should always check very carefully what it is that you are getting into.

Hire purchase

Hire purchase is still one of the most common forms of car finance. There are several important differences between hire purchase and personal loans: first, unlike a loan which can cover the whole cost, a cash deposit is normally required with hire purchase. This can also be the part exchange value of your car. Secondly, you are effectively hiring the goods rather than acquiring ownership. This means that until the final payment is made the goods do not belong to you. If you fail to make payments the gods will be repossessed.

Credit Unions

Credit unions are becoming an increasingly important low cost way of borrowing money, particularly for people who find conventional borrowing difficult to access. Essentially, credit unions are financial co-operatives set up and run by people with some sort of common bond. Members may work together or belong to the same profession or live on the same estate. The main principle is co-operation.

Members who save regularly are able to get cheap loans. Apart from the low cost you don't need an established credit record to borrow, your savings record and ability to pay will be the main factors when applying for a loan. To find out if there is a credit union you can join, or how to set one up, contact the Association of British Credit Unions.

In the chapter on savings, we discussed saving through peer-to peer lending. In this chapter, we discuss loans through peer-to peer lending

Borrowing through a Peer to Peer Platform

Over the last few years a new area of lending has been increasing in popularity – peer to peer, or social lending. The idea is that people who want to borrow money are matched up with those who will lend it.

What is peer to peer lending?

This is a form of borrowing and lending between individuals, or 'peers', without a traditional financial institution such as a bank or building society being involved. If you want to borrow money, the peer to peer websites match you up with people willing to lend it to you.As such, the companies behind these services (called 'platforms') act as intermediaries between borrowers and lenders. They can offer lower interest rates than traditional loans. Whether or not this is the case for you will depend on certain factors such as your credit rating. Some of the best deals are available only if you have an excellent credit history and no previous problems.

If you apply for a loan, you'll be credit checked using a credit reference agency and must pass the peer to peer company's own checks.

Pros of peer to peer lending

If you want to borrow some money, peer to peer loans can be cheaper than banks or building societies, especially if you have a very good credit rating. Some peer to peer websites have no minimum loan amount (in contrast to most banks and other mainstream lenders) which might suit you if you only want to borrow a small amount for a short period. They are another option if you have difficulty getting a loan from a bank or building society, depending upon your credit rating

Cons of peer to peer lending

Interest rates of peer to peer loans might be higher than high street banks or building societies, depending on your credit rating. You might have to pay a fee to the platform for arranging the loan, even if it is not fully funded. This can mean multiple fees if you have to apply more than once. You might find yourself unable to obtain a loan if you have a poor credit rating or have managed your finances poorly in the past. You might not have the same protections using a peer to peer platform as if you borrowed in other ways. This varies according to how the loans are drawn up and who the lenders are – for example, whether they are institutional investors or private individuals. Ask the platform how this works and how it differs from a normal loan.

How much do peer to peer loans cost?

The interest rates on the loans vary significantly depending on how much of a risk you're seen as. If you have a very good credit score, you might be able to borrow at an interest rate as low as around 3% but in some cases the rate might be variable, meaning the rate can go up or down each month, so you need to check.

If you have a poor credit history, your interest rate could be as high as 30% (or more likely you will be rejected). Peer to peer platforms also generally charge a fee to arrange the loans.

How do you apply for a peer to peer loan?

To apply for a loan go to one of the lending sites and register, select the amount you want to borrow and over what term. Then you can see if you'll qualify for a loan and the interest rate(s) you'll have to pay. Peer to peer lenders normally 'parcel up' the loans between lots of different people. Depending on your credit rating and the individual platform, you might be offered less than you want to borrow or you might be offered a certain amount at one interest rate and different rates of interest by other lenders.

Rules and regulations

Peer to peer platforms and some individual lenders, are regulated by the Financial Conduct Authority (FCA). That means that if you're unhappy and make a complaint, the business has eight weeks to sort it out. If, after eight weeks, you're still not happy, you can ask the Financial Ombudsman Service (FOS) to get involved. The FOS has official powers to sort out complaints between you and a financial business you're unhappy with. If they agree that the business has done something wrong, they can order them to put things right. The service is free to use. The peer2peer Finance Association (P2PFA) used to be the UK industry body for peer to peer finance and was set up to ensure high standards in this fast growing industry. However, this has now been disbanded and a new group set up. Its initial members are Funding Circle, Zopa, RateSetter, Lending Works and CrowdProperty. Membership is open to all P2P lending platforms. A good website which details these changes and more is www.p2pfinancenews.co.uk.

When applying for a peer to peer loan

Before choosing to apply for a peer to peer loan, be sure to consider:

- If you default on a peer to peer loan, the company might pass the loan on to a debt collection agency which will chase it on behalf of the lender or lenders. As a last resort, it might go to court.

- Missing payments or defaulting on a loan will affect your credit rating. Once the credit agreement is in place the peer to peer lending website will register an entry on your credit report in the same way as most other loans.

If you are turned down for credit

Lenders cannot refuse credit on factors such as race, gender or other but they can turn down your application if they think that you may not be able to repay your debt. Lenders usually make a decision as to your credit worthiness by a means of 'credit scoring' and/or by contacting a credit reference agency.

Credit scoring

Lenders score you on the basis of answers given on your application form. They take into account factors such as whether you own your home or rent, salary, age and occupation. Only those applicants who score above a certain level are deemed credit worthy.

With credit reference agencies, such as Experian and Equifax there are a number of specialist organisations which collect factual information about individuals which they pass onto lenders. Their data comes from the electoral roll, other lenders and the courts. This enables potential lenders to find out whether you have defaulted on any other credit agreements, have any County Court Judgments or are bankrupt. Negative information will stay on record for six years. If you are refused credit on the basis of information gained from an agency the lender will give you the name and address of the agency used. You can then contact the agency, with details of yourself and addresses lived in over the last six years and they will supply information. If you find that the information is incorrect then you can ask for it to be corrected and the agency must send the file to any organisation that has asked for it over the last six months.

**

Ch. 7

Income Tax Generally-How it Affects You

Income Tax

Regardless of whether we are employed or self-employed, we all have to accept the fact that HMRC are going to take a percentage of our income in the form of income tax and there is nothing we can do to avoid it.

The employed and self-employed are treated in slightly different ways and therefore we shall look at each individually, once we have assessed the structure of income tax. You should check your current tax allowances with HM Revenue and Customs as they are subject to annual change.

Personal allowance

Most people are allowed to receive a certain amount of income before tax is payable. This is known as the basic personal allowance. In 2020-21 allowances are:

Income tax: taxable bands and rates 2020/2021
England, Wales and Northern Ireland

Band	Taxable Income	Rate
Personal Allowance	Up to £12,500	0%
Basic Rate	£12501-£50,000	20%
Higher rate	£50,001-£150,000	40%
Additional rate	Over £150,000	45%

Scotland

Band	Taxable Income	Rate
Personal Allowance	Up to £12,500	0%
Starter Rate	£12,501-£14,585	19%
Basic Rate	£14,586-£25,158	20%
Intermediate Rate	£25,159-£43,430	21%
Higher Rate	£43,431-£150,000	41%
Top Rate	Over £150,000	46%

You don't get a Personal Allowance on taxable income over £125,000.

Income tax allowances

Personal Allowance and Blind Person's Allowance are fixed amounts that are set against your income, allowing you to receive that much income free of tax in any one tax year. A tax year runs from 6 April one year to 5 April the following year. **Marriage Allowance** lets you give part of your Personal Allowance to your partner, and **Married Couple's Allowance** works as a deduction from your tax bill.

Most taxpayers living in the UK on a day-to-day basis are entitled to Personal Allowance. If you're married or in a civil partnership you may be able to claim Marriage Allowance or Married Couple's Allowance as well. Some taxpayers can also claim Blind Person's Allowance.

If you have paid some tax on your income, are entitled to an allowance and are not getting it, you should claim it from HM Revenue and Customs (HMRC) by phoning the Taxes Helpline on 0300 200 3300.

If you have not received all the allowances you are entitled to, you can make a backdated claim for them. However, there is a time limit for doing this..

In practice, if you receive earnings or an occupational pension, this income is taxed through the Pay As You Earn (PAYE) system. Depending on how you are paid, every payday you will get tax-free pay of either 1/52 of your Personal Allowance if you are paid weekly, or 1/12 of your personal allowance if you are paid monthly. After taking into account any other allowances or reliefs, the amount you earn or receive as pension above this level will be taxed. This means that allowances are spread equally over the year rather than you starting to pay tax only once earnings or pensions exceed the amounts of your allowances.

What allowances are available

The following tax allowances can be given:

- Personal Allowance
- Marriage Allowance, for couples where both members were born on or after 6 April 1935, depending on how much you both earn
- Married Couple's Allowance, for couples where at least one member was born before 6 April 1935
- Blind Person's Allowance
- Personal Allowance

The Personal Allowance for the tax year 2020 to 2021 is £12,500. The Personal Allowance goes down by £1 for every £2 that your adjusted net income is above £100,000. This means the allowance is zero if income is £125,000 or above.

Marriage Allowance - if you're married or in a civil partnership

If you and your partner were both born on or after 6 April 1935, you may be able to claim Marriage Allowance. If either of you were born before 6 April 1935, you're likely to get more from Married Couple's Allowance. You can transfer £1,250 of your Personal Allowance to your spouse or civil partner if::

- your annual income is £12,500 or less
- your partner's income is between £12,501 and £50,000 (or between £12,500 and £43,430 in Scotland)
- you were born on or after 6 April 1935

This will reduce the amount of tax your partner has to pay. It will usually save them £230. You can apply for Marriage Allowance on GOV.UK.

Married Couple's Allowance

To claim Married Couple's Allowance, you must be living together as a married couple or as civil partners and at least one of you must have been born before 6 April 1935. The rules about Married Couple's Allowance depend on the date you married or became civil partners, as well as the age of the older partner: If you married before 5 December 2005, the husband gets the Married Couple's Allowance and the amount depends on the husband's income and the age of the older partner.

If you married or became civil partners on or after 5 December 2005, the partner with the higher income claims the Married Couple's Allowance and the amount depends on the age of the older partner and the income of the partner with the higher income.

If you married before 5 December 2005 you can choose to have the rules which came in on 5 December 2005 applied to you, so that the partner with the higher income gets the Married Couple's Allowance. Contact HMRC to ask them about making the change.

You can apply to HMRC to share the minimum Married Couple's Allowance between you or, if you both agree, to transfer the minimum Married Couple's Allowance to your spouse or civil partner.

You will be entitled to a Personal Allowance as well as the Married Couple's Allowance. You may also be entitled to a Blind Person's Allowance. More information about the Married Couple's Allowance is available on the GOV.UK website and on the Low Incomes Tax Reform Group's website.

Married Couple's Allowance amounts

This table gives details of the maximum and minimum Married Couple's Allowance for each year, together with the income limit. You get the maximum allowance if your income does not exceed the income limit. If your income is more than the limit, the allowance is reduced, but it won't go below the minimum amount.

Married Couple's Allowance is an amount that is taken off your tax bill, so you can only claim it if you pay tax. Your tax bill is reduced by 10% of the Married Couple's Allowance that you are entitled to. Married Couple's Allowance can't take your tax bill below £0. If it takes your tax bill to £0, any excess is not repayable. For the tax year 2020/2021 the Married Couples Allowance is:

Maximum amount	£9075
Minimum amount	£3,510
Income Limit	£30,200

More information about how income over the income limit can reduce your Married Couple's Allowance, including a calculator to see how much you may get, is available on the GOV.UK website.

Blind Person's Allowance

Blind Person's Allowance is an extra amount that can be set against set against your income, in addition to your Personal Allowance, allowing you to receive that much income free of tax in any one tax year.

In England and Wales, you can claim a Blind Person's Allowance for the whole tax year if you are registered blind with your local authority or if you become a registered blind person during the tax year. In Scotland and Northern Ireland, where there is no register, you must be unable to perform any work for which eyesight is essential. So you do not necessarily need to be completely blind to claim the allowance.

In England and Wales, HMRC can also give you the allowance in the tax year before you registered as a blind person, if you obtained the evidence needed for registration during that tax year. This may help you if there is any delay with registering as a blind person.

If you are married or have a civil partner and cannot use all of your Blind Person's Allowance, you can ask HMRC to transfer the unused part of the allowance to your spouse or civil partner. You can do this whether or not your spouse or civil partner is blind. Any surplus Married Couple's Allowance, if you qualify for it, must be transferred at the same time. If both of you are registered as blind, you can each receive the allowance. You can find more information about Blind Person's Allowance on the GOV.UK website.

Blind Person's Allowance amounts
2020/2021 tax year: £2,500

Further help with tax problems
More information about tax allowances is available on the GOV.UK website.

Allowances for older people can be complex. Go to GOV.UK for more information on personal allowances and to work out whether you should be paying tax in retirement. There is also information on tax for older people on the Low Incomes Tax Reform Group website.

If you are aged 60 or over and on a low income and have a problem with your tax allowances which you can't sort out with HMRC, you may wish to contact Tax Help for Older People www.taxvol.org.uk. Their helpline number is 01308 488066 (Monday to Friday 9am to 5pm), and you can email them from their website. They may be able to arrange a home visit if your problem is better sorted out by a face-to-face meeting.

The Employed
If you are employed your tax affairs are conducted on the fiscal year or financial year which is 6th April to 5th April the following year.

You are taxed on what is known as Schedule E (Pay As You Earn) which means that both tax and national insurance will be deducted by your employer before you receive your salary. You therefore receive your salary net of tax. This is without doubt the simplest way to conduct your tax affairs as there is very little further communication you need to have, if any, with your tax office.

At the end of the financial year you will receive a P60 which is a statement of your full year's earnings and it will contain details of how much tax and national insurance you have paid as well as pension contributions if you are in an occupational pension scheme.

You should always keep your P60 in a safe place as it often requested by banks and building societies for mortgage or loan purposes.

If you work for a large employer you may receive fringe benefits such as a company car, mortgage subsidy, or private medical insurance. These are very worthwhile benefits but you must remember they are also taxable benefits which will mean that your personal allowance will reduce to account for the real value of these benefits. If you have such benefits but notice your tax code hasn't changed then it is your responsibility to inform your tax office, as failure to do so may mean that in future years they could claim payment for undisclosed benefits.

Not all benefits are taxable, however, and the most attractive one is obviously a company pension scheme. In recent years a great deal of companies have moved towards Performance Related Pay. When you leave employment you will be provided with a P45 which is similar to a P60 but is for the benefit of your new employer to use in order to calculate your earnings to date and therefore make the necessary stoppages in your salary. It is always worthwhile taking a copy of your P45 for your own reference.

The self-employed

If you are self employed your own tax year can be any period of 12 months you want. In the eyes of the Inland Revenue you will be taxed on what is known as Schedule D and pay Class 2 National Insurance contributions.

Being self employed means that the money you receive for the services you provide will be gross and therefore no tax will have been deducted.

It is advisable that you keep an accurate record of all the money you receive and receipts for any money you spend in connection with your business activities. At the beginning of April you would normally receive a tax return form which explores all the potential sources of income you may have. This must be duly signed and returned within a month.

A large percentage of the self employed use the services of an accountant, as they best know the ways in which your tax liability can be reduced and their services certainly make it easier if you are self-employed and are hoping to take out a mortgage.

HM Revenue and Customs will negotiate with you or your accountant once they have details of your year's earnings and business expenses. Once the expenses have been taken from the gross figure this will leave your net income and therefore the amount upon which you will be expected to pay tax.

Your tax liability is normally paid in 2 installments, the first on 1st January and the second on the 1st July. The Inland Revenue, however, do not wait for your accounts to be completed and in most cases you will be expected to make installments based on assessments of your expected income and once your accounts are finalised you will then be informed of any over or under payment.

Capital Gains Tax

If you have successfully bought and sold investments, antiques and property etc., you may find that you would be liable for capital gains tax. Everyone is allowed to make a profit on opportunities that they fund with their own capital. There is, however, a limit, which you should check with HMRC, and any profit/gain that exceeds that figure would be liable for capital gains tax at the individual's marginal rate.

Tax on dividends

You may get a dividend payment if you own shares in a company. You won't pay tax on the first £2,000 of dividends that you get in the tax year. This is from 6 April to 5 April the following year. From April 2018, this has been reduced to £2,000. Above this allowance the tax you pay depends on which Income Tax band you're in. Add your income from dividends to your other taxable income when working this out. You may pay tax at more than one rate.

Tax band	Tax rate on dividends over £2,000
Basic rate	7.5%
Higher rate	32.5%
Additional rate	38.1%

Inheritance Tax

Inheritance Tax is a tax on the estate (the property, money and possessions) of someone who's died. There's normally no Inheritance Tax to pay if either:

- the value of your estate is below the £325,000 threshold
- you leave everything to your spouse or civil partner, a charity or a community amateur sports club

If you give away your home to your children (including adopted, foster or stepchildren) or grandchildren, your threshold will increase to £500,000.

If you're married or in a civil partnership and your estate is worth less than your threshold, any unused threshold can be added to your partner's threshold when you die. This means their threshold can be as much as £950,000.

Inheritance Tax rates
The standard Inheritance Tax rate is 40%. It's only charged on the part of your estate that's above the threshold.

Reliefs and exemptions
Some gifts you give while you're alive may be taxed after your death. Depending on when you gave the gift, 'taper relief' might mean the Inheritance Tax charged is less than 40%. Other reliefs, such as Business Relief, allow some assets to be passed on free of Inheritance Tax or with a reduced bill. You should contact the Inheritance Tax and probate helpline about Agricultural Relief if your estate includes a farm or woodland.

Who pays the tax to HMRC
Funds from your estate are used to pay Inheritance Tax to HM Revenue and Customs (HMRC). This is done by the person dealing with the estate (called the 'executor', if there's a will). Your beneficiaries (the people who inherit your estate) don't

normally pay tax on things they inherit. They may have related taxes to pay, for example if they get rental income from a house left to them in a will. People you give gifts to might have to pay Inheritance Tax, but only if you give away more than £325,000 and die within 7 years.

Passing on a home

You can pass a home to your husband, wife or civil partner when you die. There's no Inheritance Tax to pay if you do this. If you leave the home to another person in your will, it counts towards the value of the estate. If you leave your home to your children (including adopted, foster or stepchildren) or grandchildren, your tax-free threshold will increase to £500,000.

Giving away a home before you die

There's normally no Inheritance Tax to pay if you move out and live for another 7 years. If you want to continue living in your property after giving it away, you'll need to:

- pay rent to the new owner at the going rate (for similar local rental properties)
- pay your share of the bills
- live there for at least 7 years

You don't have to pay rent to the new owners if both the following apply:

- you only give away part of your property
- the new owners also live at the property
- If you die within 7 years

If you die within 7 years of giving away all or part of your property, your home will be treated as a gift and the 7 year rule applies.

Gifts

There's usually no Inheritance Tax to pay on small gifts you make out of your normal income, such as Christmas or birthday presents. These are known as 'exempted gifts'. There's also no Inheritance Tax to pay on gifts between spouses or civil partners. You can give them as much as you like during your lifetime, as long as they live in the UK permanently. Other gifts count towards the value of your estate.

People you give gifts to will be charged Inheritance Tax if you give away more than £325,000 in the 7 years before your death.

What counts as a gift

A gift can be:

- anything that has a value, such as money, property, possessions
- a loss in value when something's transferred, for example if you sell your house to your child for less than it's worth, the difference in value counts as a gift

Exempted gifts

You can give away £3,000 worth of gifts each tax year (6 April to 5 April) without them being added to the value of your estate. This is known as your 'annual exemption'. You can carry any unused annual exemption forward to the next year -

but only for one year. Each tax year, you can also give away:

- wedding or civil ceremony gifts of up to £1,000 per person (£2,500 for a grandchild or great-grandchild, £5,000 for a child)
- normal gifts out of your income, for example Christmas or birthday presents - you must be able to maintain your standard of living after making the gift
- payments to help with another person's living costs, such as an elderly relative or a child under 18
- gifts to charities and political parties

You can use more than one of these exemptions on the same person - for example, you could give your grandchild gifts for her birthday and wedding in the same tax year.

Small gifts up to £250
You can give as many gifts of up to £250 per person as you want during the tax year as long as you haven't used another exemption on the same person.

The 7 year rule
If there's Inheritance Tax to pay, it's charged at 40% on gifts given in the 3 years before you die. Gifts made 3 to 7 years before your death are taxed on a sliding scale known as 'taper relief'.

Years between gift and death	Tax paid
less than 3	40%
3 to 4	32%

Years between gift and death	Tax paid
4 to 5	24%
5 to 6	16%
6 to 7	8%
7 or more	0%

When someone living outside the UK dies

If your permanent home ('domicile') is abroad, Inheritance Tax is only paid on your UK assets, for example property or bank accounts you have in the UK. It's not paid on 'excluded assets' like:

- foreign currency accounts with a bank or the Post Office
- overseas pensions
- holdings in authorised unit trusts and open-ended investment companies

There are different rules if you have assets in a trust or government gilts, or you're a member of visiting armed forces.

When you won't count as living abroad

HMRC will treat you as being domiciled in the UK if you either:

- lived in the UK for 17 of the last 20 years
- had your permanent home in the UK at any time in the last 3 years of your life

Double-taxation treaties

Your executor might be able to reclaim tax through a double-taxation treaty if Inheritance Tax is charged on the same assets by the UK and the country where you lived. Gifts are not counted towards the value of your estate after 7 years. Form more help on inheritance tax rules, which can be complicated, you should contact The Inheritance Tax Helpline 0300 123 1072 or go to Gov.UK Inheritance tax.

**

Ch. 8

Funding Education

Private schools

With the huge variety of standards in education in different state schools, sometimes parents think that the only option is to educate their children privately at a fee-paying school. Fee-paying schools are used more and more by different socio-economic groups who have built up the fees through a private savings scheme. The number of fee paying schools has grown to a point where nearly 600,000 children are educated there, out of a total of 8.2 million children in receipt of education.

The state of the economy appears to have dampened the rate of increase in school fees for the first time in many years. The average annual fee for a day pupil is more than £13,000 a year – a rise of more than 3% compared with last year, but 37% higher than the £9,600 average in 2008. The impact of the 2020 pandemic has also posed a fe problems for private schools and the parents who send their children there. Nevertheless, demand will pick up and the advice in the following pages is about how best to save for educational fees.

Obviously, fee-paying schools are still going to be the preserve of those who can afford them. Fees can vary: at one end of the scale, the cheaper end, it can cost £13,000 per year per child. Indeed, there has been a growth of schools providing lower cost private education in competition with the more well known schools. At the upper end, the Eton's and Harrow's of this world, the fees are much higher. If you are intent on sending your child(ren) to a fee paying school then the only way to do so is to save from the child's early age.

If you are fortunate enough to earn enough to save for the child's education then you will be looking to invest a regular amount or a lump sum into an investment product that will, hopefully, grow at a rate higher than inflation. This could be:

- A savings account or National Savings Certificate (low risk)
- An investment or unit trust (medium to high risk)
- A bond fund (medium to low risk)
- A fixed term annuity (low risk)
- Zero preference shares

Zero preference shares are shares from an investment trust that has split itself into two types of shares. One produces capital growth but zero income. And the other just takes the income. The term 'preference shares' means that should the trust go bankrupt these shares get paid before other shares on the creditors list. You would need sound financial advice before purchasing these shares.

Your savings should be invested in as tax efficient a manner as possible, probably ISA or a children's bond. You should also be aware that gifts to a child from someone other than its parents could be tax efficient, as children have their own income tax thresholds so can earn up to that threshold without incurring tax liability.

It is recommended that parents start to invest for their children's school fees as soon as a child arrives as obviously the longer that you save the more money you will have. At pre-school and prep-school, fees are (depending on the school) lower than secondary fees and it may be possible for you to pay for them out of income and continue to contribute to a savings scheme.

Many schools offer composition fee schemes, where you start paying to the school before the child gets there. This forward paying entitles you to significant discounts from the school. However, these are only useful if your child attends that particular school. You will not receive interest on the money and will lose out if at the last moment you decide not to send your child to that school.

When advance planning for school fees there are a number of points to consider:

- It can be very disruptive to a child's education to remove them from a school where they have settled in, so make sure you can afford the fees on an ongoing basis.
- School fees tend to increase faster than the rate of inflation, so make your calculation allowing for an increase of 5% per year.
- You will need to plan for all your children. Make an assumption if you don't know how many you will have.
- Be aware of your own likely income growth.

Bursaries, scholarships and other help

Most independent schools have schemes where help is available to pay fees. They are often small amounts, amounting to several hundred pounds or less. This might make a difference however, if you are having difficulty paying fees. Scholarships are usually for more generous amounts and are awarded to children with talents deemed to be worth developing and supporting. In addition, educational trusts do exist and you might find it useful to make enquiries about these to a local education authority.

If you want more information about investing for school fees and the names of suitable advisors The Independent Schools Council can give you names of suitable firms. They can be found at www.isc.co.uk.

University education

The whole area of university funding has changed in the last 20 years or so and it is now costly to send a child to university. Most parents of children who now go to university received a grant and, other than getting part time work, received their education for free (if they went to university). Now, a contribution to education and maintenance is necessary. The burden of fees and maintenance is now largely met through student loans which only have to be repaid on leaving university. This means that the child will be liable to repay his/her own loan on leaving university. However, many parents wish to help and again a plan is necessary. The current maximum fee is £9,000 per annum with many universities charging this full amount.

Current costs of university

At current costs it is estimated that around £36,000 will be needed over a three-year period, this is without university vacations and doesn't include fees. This relates to £12,000 average per year. Some degrees can last considerably longer. It has to be remembered that costs will vary depending where you are in the UK and what university you go to. For example, studying in London will be far more expensive than studying in, say, Newcastle. The £12,000 is comprised of the following:

Rent £6000

Food and essentials £2200

Utilities and insurance £450

Travel £500

Books etc £450

Clothing and cleaning £400

Leisure £2000

It must be borne in mind that accommodation off-campus can be more expensive especially in larger cities. In out of control rent environments such as London this needs some careful thought.

Student Loan Company

The government has operated its student loan scheme through the Student Loan Company since 1990. Currently, in 2020, there is a big debate around student fees as they are the most expensive in Europe and the student loan company charges very high interest rates (no doubt because of the risk). It is hoped that change is underway to make life easier in the future for today's students. Right now, as a result of the pandemic, there is a big debate around student fees, whether they should be paid this year or not.

For more information on the loans, the terms of the loans and types of loan plus the interest rates and when and how to pay back you should go to www.slc.co.uk. There are income limits per annum before a student has to pay back the loan and nothing has to be paid back whilst studying.

As we have seen above, the outcome of a university education is that students are saddled with debt. Any help that can be given parentally is obviously a bonus. The ways of saving for university fees are the same as saving for other school fees. However, you need to be in a position where you can do this. If you are on the point of sending a child to university then you should make full enquiries to the university of choice about any extra help available if you are on a low income.

The government website www.gov.uk/student-finance also offers more information and advice on student finances.

**

Ch. 9

Financing Healthcare

Healthcare is one of the most contentious issues in modern day society, particularly now in 2020 . It is always in the news and it is used as an ongoing political football. The government tries to provide healthcare 'free at the point of delivery' and to a large extent achieves this aim. However, it is true to say that we are living longer than we used to and we are suffering more diseases and incapacities as a result. This means that the NHS has to treat more people than ever before, and there are greater pressures financially and organizationally.

Private medical care and insurance

In certain cases, it is an advantage to have private medical insurance as you will be able to exercise more choice over where and when you are treated instead of waiting in line with other people to treat what may be a painful condition. The drawback is that private medical care does not come cheap.

It is said that for people under forty, on the whole, private medical care insurance provides poor value for money. It is over the age of forty that insurance starts to provide real benefits. It is estimated that on average people in their twenties and thirties will have in-patient treatment once every ten years. The cost of that treatment averages £2000. The costs of premiums over ten years will be in the region of £7000 so the outcome is that you invest more than you get out. Of course, it may be that a serious condition occurs and that you are achieving value for money. However, it is the over-forties who tend to benefit more. Over forty though, premiums start to rise.

If you decide that you want to get private medical insurance there are certain key decisions that you might want to make. If relevant, you should see whether your employer offers such insurance. This is the cheapest option. If, however, this is not an option you will need to shop around for the best deal. Most insurance companies will offer PMI and it is usually through the larger providers of treatment such as BUPA. When selecting which level of cover is appropriate for you, you will be offered a wide range of options. The three standard areas of cover are:

- In-patient treatment (where you stay in hospital overnight or longer)
- Day-patient treatment (where you require supervised recovery time but do not stay overnight
- Out-patient treatment (where you get treatment at a consulting room or surgery)

Generally, most good policies will cover all eventualities but you may have to pay more for out-patient treatment. Other choices you will have to make are:

- Whether you wish unlimited care or a certain amount of cover each year
- Whether you wish to go to any private hospital of your choice or from a selection offered by the insurance company

- Whether cover is only offered is the NHS cannot provide cover within a given period of time (typically 6-12 weeks)
- The size of excess you are willing to pay
- The opportunity to pay for a certain part of the treatment yourself such as consultation)When applying for PMI you will be required to make a statement about your current health and any previous conditions you may have had. Failure to disclose such conditions can void your policy.

There is a standard list of conditions that insurers tend not to cover.

The Association of British Insurers lists the following:
- Pre-existing conditions
- GP services
- Long term (chronic illness)
- Accident and emergency admissions
- Drug abuse
- AIDS
- Infertility
- Normal pregnancy
- Cosmetic surgery
- Gender realignment
- Preventive treatment
- Kidney dialysis
- Mobility aids
- Experimental treatment
- Experimental drugs
- Organ transplant
- War risks
- Injuries arising from dangerous hobbies

Regulatory structure

Almost all PMI providers in the UK are members of the Association of British Insurers (ABI) and registered with the General Insurance Standards Council (GISC). You should check that your provider is registered before signing up to any scheme.

Long term care

The issue of long-term care is a relatively new one for the finance industry and is little understood by the general public. The structures of the industry and state provision are complex and there are many firms who fail to attain high standards.

Many of us will need long term care in old age. LTC comes in two forms: home care where individuals are looked after in their own homes; and care homes where people go into residential care.

Home care services range from meals on wheels, home alterations to community nursing and day care and respite centres. Local authorities provide the majority of these, but the NHS is responsible for certain areas. The NHS aid is free but usually only available when it is proved that it can improve the patient's medical condition. The general overall rule is that the majority of money is spent on those people most in need.

LTC insurance

These are 'pre-funded' policies where you purchase the cover through payment of regular premiums or with a one-off lump sum payment. You can start the policy at any age, although some insurers only offer policies to people over 40 or 50.

You will decide at the outset as to whether the policy will cover all your LTC expenses or just up to a specified amount and whether it will be a fixed level of insurance or will increase with inflation. Most policies are straightforward insurance only, but you can apply for an investment policy which will pay a capital sum at the end of the term or when you die should you have not used it in all claims. These policies tend to be more expensive. These are certain risks with LTC insurance:

- The main risk is that you may never need it and if you die before claiming or you stay healthy then the premiums will have been wasted.
- Other risks are that you are purchasing cover for some years in the future (hopefully). It is quite possible that the level of cover may be insufficient for LTC needs. Your insurance company should review the cover every five years.
- The provision of LTC insurance can affect any means tested benefits the state may provide in the future
- Certain illness and disabilities might not be covered. For example mental illness may not be covered.
- Some policies only pay out for a limited time period but most should pay as long as required. This should be checked out when taking out the policy.

The cost of LTCI will depend on age, sex and state of health when taking out the policy.

Immediate needs policies
The downside, as mentioned, of LTCI is that you may never

have to claim. Insurance companies will profit out of you. However, this is the risk with most types of insurance. An alternative to funding an ongoing policy is to take out an immediate needs policy.

Immediate needs policies are usually a variant of impaired life annuities. Life annuities are financial policies where in return for your paying a lump sum now, an insurance company guarantees to pay you a regular income each month for the rest of your life. With impaired life annuities insurers tend to be more generous as your life span is considered to be less than it should be.

There are two usual ways to pay for immediate needs policies: with a cash lump sum, or, popularly these days, with equity release. The benefits should be the same as they are determined by the annuity.

These policies are less risky than pre-funded policies as you only purchase one when you know you need it (they are not available until you have a need). However, they are more expensive as the insurance company is almost certain to have to pay you something, although it doesn't know how long. In most cases, when you have purchased an annuity you do not get money back other than the payments. As a result your estate could lose out after your death. Some policies will offer death benefits which are paid out regardless of when the policyholder dies.

Regulators, advisers and providers
The Financial Conduct Authority regulates LTCI provision. This means that all financial advisors will undergo training on LTC issues.

**

Ch.10

Paying for Weddings and Funerals

Funeral plans and over 50s plans are two different ways of paying for part of a funeral in advance. Here's what to bear in mind if you're thinking about taking one out.

Why use a funeral plan?

Many people worry that when they die, they won't leave enough money for their funeral and their loved ones will be left with the bill. With a funeral plan, you arrange and pay for it in advance, so your relatives don't have to cover all the cost themselves. You can arrange a funeral plan for your own funeral or for someone else's, as long as it's held in the UK.

With a standard funeral plan, you pay for your funeral in advance, at today's prices. You can pay the plan provider in either a lump sum or installments. You can buy a plan from most funeral directors.

Funeral plans vary in terms of what's included. All plans include the services of a funeral director who takes care of the deceased, arranges the funeral and organises transport. However, there are differences with the additional services that plans offer. Some may provide high-quality coffins, access to view the deceased in a chapel of rest, and limousines to transport guests to the funeral. Other plans may be more basic.

As well as the core costs of the funeral director and coffin, funeral plans will also include – or make a provision for – third-party costs. These can include the cost of using a crematorium, doctors' fees and the cost of a minister or celebrant. These third-party costs are usually called 'disbursements'.

If you're buying a cremation funeral plan, it won't usually cover the cost of disbursements in full. Instead, they're covered by an allowance, which rises in line with inflation. However, there's a risk that if funeral costs rise faster than inflation, there won't be quite enough money in your plan to cover these costs. This would leave your family or estate with extra to pay when you die. Some funeral plans offer a guarantee to cover all third-party costs.

If you're opting for a burial funeral plan, it will usually include the cost of digging the grave. But the cost of the burial plot – as well as extras such as headstones – won't be included.

Funeral plans never include the cost of flowers or organising a wake. But some plans allow you to put aside some extra money to cover these costs.

It's important to make sure you know what your plan does and doesn't provide before you pay.

How safe is money in a funeral plan?
Your money must either be invested in a trust fund with trustees, or in an insurance policy, which is then used to pay for the funeral.Funeral plans aren't currently regulated. But the government has announced plans to bring them under regulation by the Financial Conduct Authority.

For now, the industry relies on a voluntary regulator called the Funeral Planning Authority (FPA). They don't offer the same level of protection for customers as a government regulator, but they do have a set of standards their members have to follow. They also help to resolve customer complaints.

Make sure that you only buy plans from companies that are part of the FPA. You can check their list of members on the FPA website.

If you're paying for your funeral plan in a lump sum, you could consider paying for part of it on your credit card. When you pay with your credit card, you can get extra protection if things go wrong with the funeral director. You could also get this protection if you were to pay at least £100 on your credit card, and then pay the rest in instalments. If you die before you've finished paying the instalments, your family or estate will need to pay the balance. Some plans offer to pay the remaining instalments through a form of insurance.

Pros and cons of funeral plans
Pros:
Funeral plans give you the chance to make the arrangements that you want for your funeral. They protect you against rising costs.

Cons:
They can be expensive. Even if you're paying in instalments, they're likely to cost at least £20 a month – and often considerably more. If funeral prices fall, you could end up overpaying for your funeral. Some plans don't guarantee all the costs. Funeral plans aren't currently regulated.

Questions to ask the plan provider
- Are there any cancellation charges?
- What exactly is included in the plan and what potential costs are not?
- Could there be any other expenses for the funeral, and what happens if there are?

- Is it possible to cancel the plan if circumstances change, for example if you've arranged for your spouse's funeral but you later separate?
- Does the plan allow you to choose the funeral director?
- What if your chosen funeral director goes out of business?
- What happens if the person the funeral is intended for dies abroad or away from home?
- Can the funeral director arrange a funeral of a different standard from the one you've chosen?
- If you pay by instalments, how long do you do this for and do you have to pay interest?
- What happens if there are outstanding instalments at death?
- What freedom do you have to change the details of your funeral plan?
- How does the funeral planning company know about the plan holder's death?

Over 50s plans

Over 50s plans are insurance policies that guarantee to pay out when you die. You pay a fixed amount every month for the rest of your life. In most cases, the payout doesn't rise with inflation. They can be poor value if you live a long life – as you'll end up paying in much more than you'll get out. However, they may be right for you if you can't afford a funeral plan and you don't trust yourself to save for your funeral in a savings account, without spending the money on something else.

*

Pros and cons of over 50s plans
Pros:
Over 50s plans don't need any medical underwriting. This means that being in poor health makes no difference to your payout. You can pay as much as you can afford – unlike funeral plans where minimum premiums are much higher.

Cons:
In most cases, you lose your whole payout, and you won't get any money back, if you stop paying in the first few years. However, some providers are now offering payment holidays to give you some breathing space if you're struggling to keep up with payments. And a growing number of policies will still protect some of your payout if you stop paying after a certain number of years.

The payout on most plans doesn't increase with inflation. This means many people end up paying more in premiums than their payout. Whole of Life insurance could pay out more than 40% more when you die than an over 50s plan – according to Which?. You usually need to survive beyond the first two years of an over 50s plan to get the full payout.

Some plans require you to continue paying premiums until you die. This means that if you live a very long time, you could pay far more in premiums than you'll get back.

If you do decide to take out a funeral plan or over 50s plan, keep the paperwork in a safe place and make sure your next of kin know about it.

Alternatives to funeral plans and over 50s plans
Putting money into a savings account
Putting a little money aside each month is one straightforward way to save for a funeral. This isn't risk-free

though, as you may die before you build up enough to pay for a funeral. And many people worry that they may not have the discipline to leave their savings untouched.

Using the money you leave behind in your will

You may have assets that can be sold when you die, such as your house. You could make it clear in your will that you want these to be used to pay for your funeral. However, it can take some time for properties to be sold after someone dies. So it's worth talking to the family member who you want to arrange your funeral and checking that they have enough to pay upfront.

Death in service from an employer

Some employers provide a payout if you die while you're still working for them. If you're a member of a trade union, professional body or other association, they might pay a benefit when a member dies. Contact them to find out.

Life insurance

Using the lump sum payment from a life insurance policy can pay for a funeral. According to the Association of British Insurers, payments are generally made about a month after the policyholder dies. It could be longer if the death needs to be investigated.

More information about funerals

The sources of information differ depending on where you live:

For England and Wales, visit GOV.UK

For Northern Ireland, visit nidirect

For Scotland, visit www.mygov.scot/

In addition, Ageuk offer useful advice on planning for funerals www.ageuk.org.uk

WEDDINGS

Paying for weddings

Use your savings

This could be the cheapest option because you won't be charged interest for borrowing. Before you decide to empty your account, ask yourself these questions:

- Are you saving for a house deposit? If you're saving for a new home, consider holding onto your money because you can't use a loan or credit cards to pay for a deposit.
- What savings rate are you getting? If you can borrow interest free, you might be better off leaving your savings to earn some interest.

If you're planning your wedding day a few years in advance, you might have time to set a budget and save enough to pay for it without borrowing a penny. If you don't have any money saved up, there are other ways you can pay for your wedding.

Get a new credit card

A credit card can be an affordable way to borrow the money you need to pay for your wedding, if you're sensible.

Spread the cost and pay no interest

0% purchase credit cards let you spend without paying interest for a set number of months. for example, a card with

28 months interest free means you will not be charged any interest on anything you buy for that period as long as you meet the terms of the card. This means you can spread the cost over the interest free term, and if you pay off the balance before the term is over you can borrow interest free. However, you may only be accepted for this type of card if you have a good credit record, and the credit limit you're offered may not cover all your wedding costs.

Earn rewards

If you've managed to save the money you need to pay for your wedding, buying everything with a rewards credit card could be a great way to gain some extra perks. As long as you clear the balance in full each month with your savings, you could earn cashback, airmiles or other rewards without paying any interest. However, if you can't pay off the balance, the interest you get charged could cost you more than the perks you get in return.

Credit card spending is protected

A benefit of spending on your credit card is that it comes with protection under Section 75 of the Consumer Credit Act. Any purchase you make between £100 and £30,000 is covered, and you could get your money back from the card provider if something goes wrong.

Even if you just pay for the deposit using your credit card, the total amount will be covered under Section 75.

For example, if you paid a deposit of £100 on your credit card for your venue, and you pay off the balance of £2,500 with your savings, the total of £2,600 would be covered.

Get a personal loan

This can be an expensive way to pay for your wedding, but it could cover all your costs and let you pay it back in monthly instalments. You could borrow up to £25,000 over one to seven years with a personal loan, with some available at interest rates of less than 3%. The annual percentage rate (APR) is the interest you pay on the total value of your loan. So, the lower your APR, the less interest you'll pay on what you borrow. You should only get a loan if you don't have enough savings to cover the costs, or you can't get a 0% purchase credit card with a large enough balance.

Get help from friends and family

If you're lucky enough to have family and friends willing to help with the cost of your wedding, it can ease the strain. Traditionally, the bride's family foots the bill, but nowadays it's usually down to you to cover most of the costs. Here's more about lending money to friends and family.

Protect what you spend

Before you spend anything, think about getting a wedding insurance policy. This could cover you if something goes wrong and you have to cancel, like your venue goes out of business or one of your wedding party falls ill. However, read the policy carefully, as they vary and do not always cover what you want..

**

Ch.11

Making Money From Stocks and Shares

The investor

Individual investors can be defined as people who, after meeting all their expenses from their income have a surplus left which they wish to invest, one way or another. There are many reasons for investing, the main one being to meet future needs. Investors can keep a cash reserve in a building society or bank, they can invest in something that they think will appreciate in value, such as property, or shares which can be resold when needed.

However, right now in 2020 there are a lot of losers on the stock market due to large scale failures so do beware about investing in stocks and shares and do your homework properly. Below there are some observations on stocks and shares and the stock market generally..

Purchasing assets

Assets come in many shapes and forms, cash, premium bonds, securities such as shares in a company or gilt-edged stocks (which are government issued bonds), life assurance policies, works of art, property and so on. Each type of asset has different characteristics which will appeal to different investors.

The first characteristic of an investment that needs to be considered is an annual return: does ownership of a particular commodity entitle the investor to receive any income and if that is the case, what is the level of that income?

Income can be realised in a number of ways. There is the good old fashioned deposit in a bank or building society, which will give a monthly quarterly or annual return but not at rates that will excite the adventurous investor (particularly now). Gilt-edged bonds pay interest each year, again guaranteed but relatively low. Investment property will produce a rental income and will appreciate in value (in the good times) and the purchase of shares should, in the ideal world, produce a dividend and possibly capital growth, depending on the share. Again, like everything, the more solid the investment, as we shall see, such as in companies characterised as 'Blue Chip' companies, will generally produce stable but lower returns.

An investor will usually consider the return on an asset as an annual percentage of its value. This is the rate of return, or the yield. The rate of return on a share is known as the dividend yield and is calculated in a similar way to interest from a bank or building society: the dividend paid by a company is divided by the price of the share as quoted on the stock market. Dividend payments on shares are not guaranteed. Companies, for a variety of reasons, can decide not to pay a dividend. However, the other rate of return on shares, capital appreciation, is an equally important consideration to an investor.

Capital appreciation is the increase in value of any money invested. If inflation is higher than the rate of return then money will lose value. Shares are similar to other investments in this respect. They can fall in price as well as rise. Essentially, the total return on any asset comprises income received and the increase in value of that asset (capital growth).

Investors will need to look at the possibility of loss on

assets. Different assets have different degrees of risk, usually relating to their potential for appreciation or depreciation. Deposits in banks will rarely if ever depreciate as periodic interest will be added and the investment will be protected apart from a possible loss of value due to inflation.

Ordinary shares carry risks of both falling prices and falling returns. A company's declining profits can result in a fall in the share price and also lead to a company deciding not to pay dividends. Many investors will usually try to create a portfolio of shares, ranging from more high-risk equities to safer homes, so that a fall in the value of one is offset by the growth in value of another.

Basically, different assets have different degrees of return. The main principle is that the higher the return the higher the risk.

Investors will also take into account the degree of ease with which they can convert their asset into cash if need arises. This is known as the liquidity of an asset. The liquidity of an asset will affect the return received. The more liquid an asset, as a general principle, the lower the return. Asset liquidity and asset values are also affected by time. For example, the longer that money is tied up in a bank account the more illiquid that it is. Because of uncertainty about the future, money today is worth more than money tomorrow. To bring their values into balance, and to encourage saving and investing rather than spending, the longer that money is unavailable in the present, the greater the reward.

Hedging and speculation

When weighing up which assets to buy or to hold, an investor will keep coming back to the main consideration: risk. The more risk-averse investor will want as much protection of their assets value as possible. There are various means of achieving this. One basic strategy is called hedging, and it is a version of the strategy of portfolio diversification: the investor will hold two or more assets whose risk/return characteristics to some degree offset each other. One typical example is to hold one safe but low return asset for one high-risk one.

A more precise way to hedge is to use derivatives, the range of securities whose price depends on or derives from the price of an underlying security. A put-option, for example, gives its owner the right, but not the obligation, to sell a share at a fixed price (the striking price) on or at a certain date. Owning a put option with the share itself means that the investor's potential capital loss is limited to the loss implied should the share fall to the striking price.

If it falls further the investor can use the option and sell at the striking price.

The speculator

On the other side of the hedgers trading is the speculator. This is someone who is prepared to take on the extra risk that the hedger wants to avoid. Speculators are in the market with the intention of making as much money as possible. They believe that they know the future prospects for asset prices better than the majority of investors, and hence are prepared to take bigger risks. Investors, whether hedgers or speculators, who expect a rise in a particular asset price or in the market as a whole are known as bulls, whilst those who express pessimism about the future of the markets are known as bears.

Markets

Assets are bought and sold in markets. Markets are institutions that allow buyers and sellers to trade assets with one another through the discovery of prices with which both are satisfied. Some traders may meet in physical places. However, in the age of technology, and the pandemic, this is not necessary or possible. Wherever and however the trading is carried out, what is actually happening is a form of auction. For example a trader may have 100 lots of assets to sell. If there are more or less traders at the suggested price (more or less than 100) the trader will lower or raise the price accordingly. This becomes the current market price.

Financial markets can be classified in different ways. One basic distinction is between primary and secondary markets. In primary markets, new money flows from lenders to borrowers as companies and governments seek new funds. In secondary markets investors buy and sell existing assets among themselves. The existence of the secondary market is generally considered to be essential for a good primary market. The more liquid the secondary market, the easier it should be to raise capital in the primary market by persuading investors to take on new assets. The secondary market allows them to sell should they decide that it is an asset that they don't want to hold. Markets may also be classified by whether or not they are organised, whether they are regulated by an institution. For example, the London Stock Exchange is an organised market while the over-the-counter derivatives market is not.

Markets can be classified by the nature of the assets traded on them: stocks, bonds, derivatives, currencies, commodities and so on. All of these are distinct markets and there are strong connections between them. These connections grow stronger as increasing globalisation and improved technology allows better flows of information. An investor will need this diverse but interlinked information to allow them to compare and contrast different investments.

How The Stock Market Works-what is a stock market?

Most people know a market, in the broadest sense, as a number of stalls, trading outdoors, from which you can buy almost any commodity. You can buy fruit and vegetables, clothing, travel goods and so on at an outdoor market. There will be the usual smattering of Del boys and Arthur Daly's. A stock market has the same features, buyers and sellers, an agreed price (with the same smattering of sharp characters). However in stock markets you will usually also have a middleman, essential to guide the investor through the maze of dealings on offer, known as a stockbroker. More about brokers later.

There are many recordings of the first known stock markets in European Cities. In Britain, the first recorded joint stock company was founded in 1553 to finance an expedition to the orient, via a northeast passage. Two of the ships sheltered from storms in Scandinavia and all the crew froze to death. The third reached Archangel and then went overland to Moscow-which was as near to the Orient as they got, and agreed a trading link with The Czar Ivan the Terrible.

There have been many similar ventures. Alongside these ventures London's financial institutions grew. The London Stock Exchange grew out of a small coffee house-the New Jonathans Coffee rooms. As the business grew they moved and eventually in 1801 acquired the name the London Stock Exchange. There used to be a number of stock exchanges dotted around the country but they were eventually amalgamated into one exchange in Old Broad Street London, next to the Bank of England. The stock exchange has since moved as it has had to increase its space as time has moved on and technology and the world markets have grown more complex.

There are two elements to the London Stock Exchange, the first being the official list, which is the main market of the major companies. This is further divided up into groupings by trade. There is a section for distribution, banks, breweries plus one for Techmark (or techMark as it is known) for high-tech companies. In addition there is the Alternative Investment Market (AIM) which is for young companies that do not have the trading record demanded for a full listing. See below for more information.

Stock markets now are remote from companies and deal electronically. London's main market operates on a computerised system called the Stock Exchange Electronic Trading System (SETS) for large shares, with a modified version for mid-market companies. SETS is an order matching system that pairs off the instructions sent to the machine by buyers and sellers. Some stocks are traded using a system called SEAQ (Stock Exchange Automated Quotation System), which is based on an American system. The completed deal is passed to another computer to organize settlement.

The Crest system is trying to eliminate the mass of paper by replacing share certificates with an electronic record. Share certificates are still available for those who want them.

Other UK markets-The Alternative Investment Market (AIM)

AIM is usually known by its initials and is a division of the stock market reserved for small businesses. The idea is that the smaller business will grow and mature and graduate to a full listing. The costs of listing on AIM are almost as high as a full listing. However, the hurdles for acceptance on the AIM are lower. There are about 750 companies from a variety of countries listed and the number is growing. For the smaller investor in Britain there is an added attraction in that Aim listed companies are regarded by Her Majesty's Revenue and Customs as unquoted, thus providing access to differing tax relief schemes, including business taper and gift relief for capital gains tax, suitability for the Enterprise Investment Scheme, relief for losses and business property relief for inheritance tax (see section on tax further on in the book). The downside, and there always is one, is that smaller companies are less secure and more vulnerable to financial problems

TechMark

TechMARK and techMARK mediscience are specially developed segments of the London Stock Exchange's Main Market, designed for companies at the forefront of innovative technology.

TechMARK was launched in November 1999 by the Exchange to create new opportunities for companies whose business is dependent on technological innovation, and for investors in those companies. Two years later, techMARK mediscience was then launched to focus on companies whose business is dependent on innovation in the development or manufacture of pharmaceuticals, or products or services that are wholly or substantially dedicated to the healthcare industry.

TechMARK brings together companies whose business models require a particularly high level of innovation and investment into research and development programmes. By providing a spotlight on this segment of the Main Market, it helps techMARK companies to build successful relationships with investors – vital to innovation and funding discovery.

And for scientific-research based companies, the Listing Rules take into account business specialisation and facilitate admission to the Main Market.

Who can join?

TechMARK is open to all innovative companies, regardless of size, sector or commercial or industrial activity, country of origin or currency of share trading. There is a broad range of companies operating in numerous sectors on techMARK, from software and computer services to oil and gas and even transport. TechMARK mediscience companies operate within the techMARK family. TechMARK mediscience specifically includes healthcare sectors such as medical equipment, medical supplies, biotechnology and pharmaceuticals. All techMARK companies share one key attribute – commitment to innovation, research and development.

OFEX

OFEX provides a market for the securities of smaller companies. Currently, OFEX has approximately 140 companies traded, representing 25 industry sectors. It has served over 500 companies, out of which over 90 companies have used OFEX as a stepping-stone to more senior markets such as AIM or the Official List of the London Stock Exchange. Companies on the OFEX market have raised in excess of GBP1.10bn, using the broad membership of corporate advisers and broker/dealers.

Information relating to OFEX companies can be access on the corporate website, www.ofex.com. Under the .company data. section of the website investors can access free of charge real-time trading and share price information of all OFEX securities, all news published by our companies, as well as reports and accounts.

Virt X

This incorporates a small rival to the London Stock Exchange called Tradepoint, which started as an electronic order book in 1995 and was itself quoted on AIM. In combination with the Swiss Stock Exchange SWX, it created Virt X, with offices in London and Zurich although all trading is carried out from Zurich. In addition to trading in the normal UK quoted stocks, it has set up clearance and registry systems to allow trading in Eurotop, the 300 largest companies in Europe.

General points about trading on the stock markets

What does the existence of these multiple trading markets mean to the small investor? It means two things. It means that you have easier access to trade shares of companies beyond those that are listed and traded on the London Stock Exchange. A customers order can be routed to any FSA authorised market where the security trades. Each brokerage firm decides where to route the buy and sell orders it handles.

A brokerage firm tries to get the best price for its customer. This means executing an order to buy securities (stocks, bonds, ETF's (exchange traded funds-more later) etc at the lowest price available at the time the order reached the trading market. When a customer places an order to sell, the brokerage firm tries to execute the order at the highest price available.

The basic order types

It is important to understand the meaning of the different types of buy and sell orders used by brokers to get a trade executed in a specific way. Basically, unless you have an idea of what stock brokers are talking about you will find yourself at a disadvantage.

A typical small investor will find that five basic order types will serve most of their investment needs:

- A market order
- A limit order
- A marketable limit order
- A stop order
- A stop-limit order

It is important to understand how each order works and the possible result associated with using each. One basic feature of orders must be clearly understood first. When an order ticket is marked it can be marked in one of four ways:

BUY

'BUY' means the investor is acquiring a securities position with the expectation that the price will rise over time. The words ' Buy' and 'Long' are synonyms in the investment market.

SELL LONG

Order tickets are not simply marked 'sell'. Each ticket must specify whether it is an order to 'sell long' or 'sell short'. Sell long means an investor is selling securities that they already own.

SELL SHORT

'Sell short' is more complicated. It means that the investor is selling securities that he or she does not own. In fact, the securities that are being sold short have been borrowed on the investors behalf by the brokerage firm. The investor is expecting the market price of the securities to decline over the short term so they can buy them back at a lower price. The difference between the higher price at which the securities are initially sold short and the lower price at which they are eventually bought back is the profit to the investor. Needless to say, for the small investor this is a route that is better left alone.

BUY TO COVER

'Buy to cover' means the investor is liquidating a short position. In reality, when the brokerage firm gets this order it buys back the securities that were sold short for the investor. Remember, the brokerage firm had borrowed the securities for the customer. Now it returns these to the lender, which is usually another brokerage firm.

The five basic order types-*A market order*

A market order, whether placed with a broker or using an electronic order ticket, contains only the name of the security and the amount in pounds. It does not specify a price or time, as the examples below illustrate:

buy £1,000 of BT -or- Sell £1,000 of Vodafone

A market order must be executed immediately at the BBO, best bid price or offer price, available in the market at that time.

Limit Order

When placing a limit order, the investor specifies the price at which he or she wants to buy a specific security.

For example:

Sell £1,000 of Shell at 1.39p -or- Buy £1,000 of Mears Group at 500p

Importantly, when a limit order is placed, it is understood that the order will be executed only at the specified price or better. the investor who wants to sell wants 1.39p or better. Those who want to sell or want to buy want a certain price or lower.

Marketable limit order

This is a variation on the limit order that is used on many of the computerised order-matching systems. Unlike a traditional limit order, which is entered below or above the market, a marketable limit order is entered at the current price level at which a share is trading. In placing this order, a customer is making sure that the order will be executed only at the current price level or better.

If, for example, a share is trading at 660p and you want to buy shares at this price only, you would enter a marketable limit order with a specified price of 660p. Your order would be eligible for immediate execution. The advantage of a marketable limit order is that if the share price unexpectedly moved above 660p, then your order would not be executed. If the share price moved lower then your order would be executed because the lower price is better than the specified price.

Stop order

Like a limit order, an investor must specify a price, called the stop price, when the order is placed. However, with a stop order, when the security's price hits the specified price, the order is transformed into a market order, and is executed at the security's current BBO, whatever that may be. This is the most useful order for investors who want to limit losses and protect profits. The example below illustrates this.

Let's say that you have just bought a company's shares, which are trading at 660p. When you buy these shares you are, of course, concerned that the price might decline suddenly, resulting in a significant loss. To limit your potential loss you place a sell stop order at 640p, below the price at which you bought the stock. It is important to understand that the price that you specify on a sell stop order is only a trigger. If the share price suddenly plummets and hits your 640p price, the order is immediately transformed into a market order. Subsequently, it is executed at whatever the market price might be at the moment, which may be above or below the stop price. In this case, the sell stop order would limit your loss on the position to around 20p. The loss could be greater if the share price is in free fall.

Stop limit order

When an investor places a stop limit order, he or she must specify a stop price and a limit price. For example:
Sell £1,000 of Costain at 3.20p stop 3.50 limit
-or- But £1,000 of Mears at 500p 520 limit

On a sell stop limit order, the limit price is the same or lower than the stop price and on a buy stop limit order the limit price will be the same or higher than the stop price.

Although some of the above may sound a little confusing, especially for the first time investor, it is worthwhile knowing the basics of share sale or purchase terminology.

**

Ch. 12

The Benefits of Owning Shares

When looking at shares as opposed to other savings investments, it has to be said that the number of ways a person can invest amounts of their hard earned cash is limited.

There are a whole range of savings accounts paying varying rates of interest, ranging from mediocre to high, all dependant on what you want for the future of your savings, i.e. instant access, long term growth and so on.

Property has proved to be a good investment over the years, particularly with the advent of buy-to-let mortgages. An investor can realise an income and also growth in capital value. However, this type of investment is not for everyone, particularly because of the high capital investment at the outset.

Art is another area of investment but again not suitable for everyone as it requires specialist knowledge when purchasing in order to ensure capital growth.

There are a whole range of other collectibles which rely on at least a basic level of knowledge at the outset. Wine is one area and antiques another.

Because most people need access to their capital to fund a whole range of short and longer term projects, such as holidays, education and so on, buying shares usually ranks way down the list as an investment.

Shares are usually a longer-term investment and the risk involved in the investment depends on the timescale of that investment. Rewards can be measured more easily if a longer term has been allowed to elapse.

The stock market provides a fairly good home for investments for those people who are prepared to accept a degree of risk and can wait for the right moment before cashing in and pulling out. Essentially, money invested in the stock market should not be money that you need to realize at short notice or money that will be realized for your old age. The stock market is only for people who have spare cash to invest and can weather the storm if a loss is made. It is not for those who will lay awake at night worrying about losing money on shares.

If you do decide to invest in the stock market, and there are about 12 million people who have done so in the U.K. then don't put everything you have to invest in the market at once. Keep some aside to invest when a really good opportunity arises.

There are two ways to invest in the stock market, long term (suitable for the small investor) and as an active trader.

Long-term investment

It is true to say that in the long term the stock market has produced a better return on investment than any other alternative form of investment. All of the charts produced to indicate growth have demonstrated that over a period of 30, 50 and more years, returns from shares outperform most other investments. Shares in Britain have, since 1918, produced a return of over 12% a year compared with other investments such as government issued gilt edged securities which have produced just over 6%.

This return on shares has been in the face of the periodic cyclical downturns in the economy and in overseas economies. Cash in a deposit account would have produced 5% in the same period. However, cash in a deposit account is safe and as we have seen shares can be a risk.

When considering the long term, questions of future economic stability will always arise. For sure, at different periods economies will fluctuate and losses will occur but in the longer term these tend to even out and share prices rise, as history has demonstrated.

It is up to the investor to decide what they want from an investment. Do you want income or capital growth? These are not absolute alternatives, since companies that do well hand out handsome dividends (usually) and see their share price rise. Unit trusts and investment trusts as we have seen provide good homes for savings and, at the very least will ensure inflationary growth.

Short-term investments

This is another way of investing, but it is for the experts and people who are sufficiently clued up and will devote time to study the markets. This is the short-term active trading which is built on the tactic of taking advantage whenever share prices move sharply enough to make trading beneficial. The active short-term trader will watch the markets very carefully and look for opportunities such as takeovers and mergers where they can buy and sell relatively quickly at a profit.

Short-term investing usually requires more money than longer term investing as the costs of trading can be higher as brokers fees and government taxes have to be paid.

Perks of owning shares

In addition to the usual benefits of owning shares, such as appreciation of capital and dividend income, many companies try to keep shareholders loyal by offering perks, usually in the form of discounts of one form or another. Channel tunnel has travel concessions offered to shareholders, other nationally known companies such as Iceland and Kwik Fit all provide benefits to investors. A number of fund managers will provide a list of companies that provide perks for shareholders.

How to Buy Shares and Taxation on Shares

When considering the initial amount to invest in a parcel of shares, it is important to realise that the less you invest the higher the overall cost of shares, because of fees etc, and the more a share has to rise to make a decent return. It is for this reason that most people in an advisory capacity would say that £2,000 is the minimum that should be invested.

For safety the investment should be spread over a number of companies. The old adage 'don't put all of your eggs in one basket' rings very true here. A common portfolio for a small investor should contain at least 12 companies (but not more as the other factor is that the investor should stay in control of his or her investments).

The main aim of all investing is to get a decent return with the minimum acceptable risk. If you own shares in one company then the risk and possibility of losing your money is greater than if the risk is spread.

It is a general rule that the lower the risk the lower the return. However, the converse holds true, the higher the risk the higher the return. For some people who invest in a single company the rewards can be big if the company does well. In truth what usually happens is that large investments in one company will not produce massive returns or result in loss of all ones investment. The shares will usually carry on rising marginally in the longer term.

Buying through Investments Trusts-Purchasing unit trusts

There are benefits connected to the purchase of unit trusts and investment trusts as opposed to individual shares. With trusts you get a spread of investments over a number of companies, cutting the danger of one of the companies going out of business.

Investment trusts

Investment trusts are companies which invest in other companies on behalf of investors. They are termed close-end funds because the number of shares on issue is fixed and does not fluctuate no matter how popular the fund may be. This sort of investment is convenient for small investors who do not have enough money to buy a lot of shares in different companies thereby spreading the risk. An investment trust will have its money spread across a lot of companies so problems with one company will usually be compensated by a boom in another company. Managers of investment trusts are professionals, so, at least in theory, they will do better than the average person. It is true to say that investment companies are as good as their managers so it is wise to pick a company with a good and known track record.

Most investment funds have a lot of money to invest and they will usually invest in blue chip shares, unless specifically set up to invest in a specific type of share.

The cost of the stockbroker is the same as it would be with other dealings and the government stamp duty and the price spread between buying and selling price remains the same.

Although investment trust managers do have a lot of say in the nature and type of investments, investors will also have some say in what goes on by buying the right investment trust shares. There are trusts specializing in the higher risk stock markets such as Budapest, Istanbul and Madrid (called emerging markets); there are some investing in the Pacific Rim and some concentrating in Japan; some go for small companies and some specialize in Europe and the United States and so on. The spread of investments can be very diverse indeed and managers of investment trusts tend to be more adventurous on the whole than managers of unit trusts.

Some trusts are split capital trusts which have a finite life during which one class of share gets all the income, and when it is wound up the other class of share gets the proceeds from selling off the holdings.

Trusts are quoted on the Stock Exchange so the share price can be tracked and also the asset value of the trust can be calculated. The asset value is comprised of the value of the shares that the trust is holding compared with the trusts own share price. One main reason that many are priced differently than their real value is that major investing institutions avoid trusts. Huge pension funds or insurance companies do not have to buy in to investment expertise as they normally have their own experts. Therefore trusts are used mainly by private investors.

Unit trusts

Unit trusts have the same advantage of spreading risk over a large number of companies and of having the portfolio of shares managed by professionals. However, instead of the units being quoted on the stock market as investment trusts are, investors deal directly with the management company. Therefore the paper issued has no secondary market. The investor cannot sell to anyone other than back to the management company. The market is seen from the manager's viewpoint: it sells units at the offer price and buys them back at the lower 'bid' price, to give it a profit from the spread as well as the management charge. Many unit trust prices are published in quality papers.

These are called 'open-ended' funds, because they are the pooled resources of all investors. If more people want to get into a unit trust it will issue more paper to accommodate them. Unlike the price of investment trust shares, which is set by market demand and can get totally out of line with the market value the price of units is set strictly by the value of shares the trust owns.

Tracker funds

Tracker funds move with the main stock market index, in the U.K that is usually taken to be the FTSE 100. This type of fund is for the less adventurous investor who looks for a virtually risk free return.

Open-ended investment companies

Open Ended Investment companies or OEICs are placed midway between investment trusts and unit trusts. They are incorporated companies and issue shares, like investment companies.

Like unit trusts the number of shares on issue depends on how much money investors want to put into the fund. When money is taken out and shares sold back, those shares are cancelled. The companies usually contain a number of shares segmented by specialism.

This enables investors to pick the area they prefer and to switch from one fund to another with a minimum of administration and cost.

Advantages of pooled investments

Pooled investments reduce risk and are therefore a safer home for small investors. However, as they are safe they are unlikely to hit the outside chance of a high performer, as individual share speculators might.

As stated earlier, there are many different companies and a certain degree of research and knowledge is essential before committing. To be forewarned is to be forearmed. Quality newspapers will have regular league tables of performance.

Be careful too with tables that are published showing performance. Obviously, tables can only look backwards to demonstrate past performance and it is the future that matters. Trusts can do very well, but it may be that they have done well in a sector that has expanded and is now contracting.

Management charges for both investment trusts and unit trusts are usually high. One way of avoiding high charges is to opt for a U.S. mutual fund, which is the same as a unit trust and which has lower charges.

There is also the alternative of setting up your own investment vehicle which has become quite popular over the years. Investment clubs, described below, already very popular in the United States are growing more popular up in the U.K. Basically, a group of people together pool cash for investment in the stock market. The usual way is for each member to set aside a regular amount each month and decide where to invest it. This has the advantages of avoiding charges, spreading investments and also the social spin off. Also, the work of researching shares is spread amongst members.

Exchange traded funds

Exchange-traded funds, or ETFs, are investment companies that are legally classified as open-end companies or Unit Investment Trusts (UITs), but that differ from traditional open-end companies and UITs in the following respects:

- ETFs do not sell individual shares directly to investors and only issue their shares in large blocks (blocks of 50,000 shares, for example) that are known as "Creation Units."
- Investors generally do not purchase Creation Units with cash. Instead, they buy Creation Units with a basket of securities that generally mirrors the ETF's portfolio. Those who purchase Creation Units are frequently institutions.
- After purchasing a Creation Unit, an investor often splits it up and sells the individual shares on a secondary market. This permits other investors to purchase individual shares (instead of Creation Units).
- Investors who want to sell their ETF shares have two options: (1) they can sell individual shares to other investors on the secondary market, or (2) they can sell the Creation Units back to the ETF. In addition, ETFs generally redeem Creation Units by giving investors the securities that comprise the portfolio instead of cash. So, for example, an ETF invested in the stocks contained in the Dow Jones Industrial Average (DJIA) would give a redeeming shareholder the actual securities that constitute the DJIA instead of cash. Because of the limited redeemability of ETF shares, ETFs are not considered to be—and may not call themselves—mutual funds.

An ETF, like any other type of investment company, will have a prospectus. All investors that purchase Creation Units receive a prospectus. Some ETFs may furnish an investor with a summary prospectus containing key information about the ETF instead of a long-form prospectus. If an investor receives a summary prospectus, the ETF's long-form prospectus will be available on an Internet Web site, and an investor can obtain a paper copy upon request and without charge. Some broker-dealers also deliver a prospectus to secondary market purchasers. ETFs that do not deliver a prospectus are required to give investors a document known as a Product Description, which summarizes key information about the ETF and explains how to obtain a prospectus. All ETFs will deliver a prospectus upon request. Before purchasing ETF shares, you should carefully read all of an ETF's available information, including its prospectus.

The websites of the New York Stock Exchange and NASDAQ provide more information about different types of ETFs and how they work. An ETF will have annual operating expenses and may also impose certain shareholders fees that are disclosed in the prospectus.

Investment clubs

Investment clubs are an alternative to funds managed by professionals and as a result can keep costs down. Investment clubs are a group of private investors who pool their money and decide collectively how it should be invested. There are now over 7,000 investment clubs in the U.K.

The ideal number of people in an investment club is usually between 4-20. If the membership exceeds 20 then HMRC will term the club a corporation and corporation tax will be payable. There are several stockbrokers, including major banks who have ready-made packages for investment clubs, such as Barclays and Nat West.

There is a specialist charity called pro-share which publishes a handbook on how to start an investment club. The advice contained in this handbook is very useful indeed because, although it is not absolutely necessary to have an in-depth knowledge of the stock market when joining an investment club it is at least useful to know something about the different sectors that you will be investing in.

For investors clubs there are model rules and constitutions that need to be adopted. As with all collective endeavours, from residents associations to enthusiasts clubs, rules and guidelines are essential. Investment club rules will set out, for example, how members can join and leave the club, a unit valuation system that is to be adopted, the decision making process, levels of monthly subscription, meetings, appointment of officers and so on. It is of the utmost importance that procedures are followed as disaster will almost certainly ensue. It is important to look at whether the club will run indefinitely, accumulating a portfolio or whether it has a specific life, say 5 years. An investor might be invited to join an existing club so it is important that these rules are already in place and that they are the right ones for you.

A few other tips. Only join in with people that you like and trust. Ensure that their objectives and goals are the same as yours or it could end in tears later down the line. The criteria for choosing investments varies widely from club to club but many will go for the riskier end of the market because the club membership is additional to a members own personal investments. Some investment clubs will go beyond the stock market and invest in property either directly or indirectly through another vehicle.

The main advice given to any club member or would-be member is not to invest in anything that you do not understand. Avoid the overly complex and riskier markets such as derivatives, unless you have an expert on board.

Most clubs invest a small sum, it could be under £80 per month, so this type of investing is just as much fun, and social, as it is serious money making. There are some investment clubs who have had runaway success but, on the whole it is for the smaller investor with other aims in mind.

The cost of dealing in shares as an individual

Share dealing can be expensive, particularly in Britain. It is the case that it is more expensive here than in many other countries, and also the whole process is more complex, at least for individual shareholders. True, there have been moves by high street banks and other companies to make the process more transparent but it is still the case that small shareholders find the process rather confusing. It is also the case that small shareholders are still perceived to be a nuisance, because they deal in small amounts of money which cost just as much to transact as larger deals.

Commission

Commission paid to stockbrokers constitutes the main cost of dealing in shares. Commissions vary depending on the nature of the work and the type of broker. Rates of commission can vary anything from £5 per transaction up to £20 with commission on a sliding scale above the minimum depending on the value of the transaction. An order of £2,000 might cost 1.5% with the rate falling the higher the transaction. There can also be a one-off charge of at least £10 for joining Crest, the UK stock exchanges registry of share holdings.

There are several internet sites, such as www.fool.co.uk which provide information about brokers commissions. It is worth looking at this site before going ahead.

Robo-advisors

Would you trust an algorithm to look after your investments? Hundreds of thousands of investors do, using robo-adviser. These are investment platforms that provide algorithm-based services to automate parts of the investment process. Technology is used to reduce the complexity and lower the costs often associated with investing. Robo-advisers claim to provide a low-cost, flexible and efficient alternative to the traditional wealth management industry. Among the names to know are Nutmeg and Wealthify. You will usually be asked 10 or 15 simple questions, after which you are shown a suitable basket of investments. Once you agree, the platform manages these investments for you. Charges tend to be no more than 1 per cent and can be as low as 0.6 per cent. Nutmeg is the biggest of the robo-advisers, with more than £2billion of investors' savings in its coffers. Investors choose from ten fully managed (by a team of human managers) portfolios or five unmanaged ones (updated by algorithms) and charges are up to 1 per cent or 0.68 per cent for unmanaged. Nutmeg requires a minimum £500 deposit for an Isa, pension or investment account with just £1. Wealthify offers five risk categories and will let you start investing from just £1. It charges 0.6 per cent. The downside of robo-advice is that it is a very broad approach. Not everyone's risk tolerance fits into fixed categories and, as life goes on, financial circumstances tend to get far more complicated. During difficult times, a robo-adviser would be unlikely to rival the decisions made by a seasoned investor or adviser.

Some of the savings apps, including Plum, will automatically invest your savings, buy you choice of funds is usually very limited.

The spread

As well as brokers commission there is the cost of trading. Shares are like other commodities, the costs of buying and selling shares will differ. This difference is known as the 'spread'. Spread varies with risk. Big companies listed on the FTSE 100, such as Barclays, British Airways etc have huge market capitalisations and many shareholders with regular deals every day so would have a narrow spread of say 1-1.5%. A company with few shareholders and little trade would have a spread of up to 10%. The result is that for shareholders of small companies the shares have to rise even higher to realise a profit. There is lots of free advice concerning shares. However, it is true to say that for the small, first time investor even free advice can be confusing and misleading, given that this advice is often slanted in favour of whoever gives it. It is therefore advisable to use a stockbroker who is seasoned and knows the markets well.

For those with a larger share portfolio it is possible to sub-contract out the management. The stockbroker managing the portfolio will advise on investments but leave the final decision to the investor. The value of portfolios has to be high however, and this will not usually be the route for small investors. In addition to portfolio management there is discretionary management where a fee is paid to an advisor to provide advice on shares and also the timing of share purchase. The fee paid is quite high, or is based on a percentage and is therefore only useful for those with bigger portfolios.

Income tax

Another consideration to take into account, after everyone has taken their cut, is that of the ever-present HMRC. The government will take its cut by imposing a tax called stamp duty at the rate of .5% on the value of every deal that has used taxed income. The French and German governments do not impose such a tax therefore money can be saved by investing through these exchanges.

Buying shares

The process of buying shares has become markedly easier over the last few decades. In fact, many people have acquired shares through privatisations and through building societies becoming banks, and have not had to use a stockbroker. However, if people want to buy shares in the usual way there are several routes.

The first one is finding a stockbroker. Years ago, this was out of the reach of the small investor. Most stockbrokers operated within exclusive circles. Many did not want to be bothered with the small investor who knew very little, if anything about the markets. Banks have entered the arena with share dealing services and so has a new breed of transaction only brokers (who buy and sell but do not offer advice). However, more and more information is becoming available, through the internet and in newspapers. There has been a trend to present information in a plain English way and the information regarding shares is no different. Finding a broker over the internet is probably the easiest way to get started.

The internet has undermined the closed nature of share dealing and there are a large number of independent companies, most of which are members of The Association Of

Private Client Investment Managers and Stockbrokers (see useful addresses). Many have their own web sites.

There are three main types of broker, each offering a differing array of services: execution-only brokers; advisory brokers; discretionary brokers.

Execution only brokers

Execution-only brokers will simply handle the sale or purchase of shares at your request, whether this is carried out online or on the phone. They do not offer investment advice. The firms computer routes your order to the market where the shares are trading and it will simply execute your order at the best possible price. The broker will receive a commission on each transaction.

Advisory brokers

As the name suggests, an advisory broker will offer the best advice and strategies for you to increase the value of your investment portfolio and achieve your investment aims. This type of broker will try to get to know you and to gain a clearer idea of your aims. An advisory broker will be more expensive than an execution only broker, because of the more intensive nature of their service, but if you take advantage of the expert advice on offer then it will be worthwhile.

Discretionary brokers

This type of broker will have written authority from you or someone acting on your behalf to decide what securities can be bought and sold on your account.

For most new investors who may not be very knowledgeable about the markets or investing, it is generally safer to go with an advisory broker who can help you through the maze and also help to maximise the value of your investments.

People who think that they need help and advice can go to one of the big high street financial institutions with branches round the country. They can also seek out a good local firm that is experienced in the needs of small investors. The best way to find such a firm is by recommendation (like a lot of things) or you can go to the Association of Private Client Investment Managers and Stockbrokers.

Before picking a broker, ask questions such as how easily contactable are they and other terms and conditions.

Buying Shares Over The Internet

Internet broking has, like many other activities on the internet, grown massively. The internet has a lot of real advantages. Investors can place an order whenever they feel ready and can do it from any place any time. In addition, an enormous amount of information is available online to assist with decision making.

Dealing on the internet can also be cheaper. It is possible to deal over the net for a flat fee of around £10, although this varies. This is important for those who plan to be active investors and to whom the fees paid are crucial to profit margins. One Paris based research outfit called Blue Sky reckons that the four best value online brokers are all German.

www.money.co.uk/share-dealing.htm is a good place to start for information about share dealing over the internet and it will also give you a breakdown of current share prices and fees.

One acknowledged problem with the web is that it is hard to get a picture of the reliability of the firm that you are dealing with. The web is largely faceless so there are risks of various sorts, such as hacking into your data and so on. Online trading does not generate a share certificate. The shares are registered to the new owner but it is still computerised and the broker will hold the title to them in a nominee account. This can mean that the investor cannot easily change allegiance to another broker.

To join an online stockbroker, you need to get on to a website and follow instructions for registering. Almost all will require cash deposited with the brokerage. Interest is paid on this money at a low rate. When signing on you register a password which provides secure access for the investor.

If you want to invest in the US you might want to go through a US based broker. These brokers are cheaper than European counterparts.

There are two sorts of dealing online: one is to e-mail an instruction to a broker who will execute it via his trading screen. In theory he can do that within 15 seconds and within 15 minutes the deal can be confirmed. The other method is called real time dealing in which the investor connects directly to the stock market dealing system.

Normally, when the instruction is given, the broker will 'transact at best'-buy at the lowest available price and sell at the highest. The broker can be set a limit-the maximum at which you are prepared to buy or the minimum price below which you are not prepared to sell. Usually, such limits last for 24 hours although can be longer.

Once the transaction is complete the broker sends a contract note detailing the deal and how much money is to change hands. It may take some time to receive the share certificate but the important element is the presence on the share register.

Taxation and Shares

The area of tax and share dealing has always been a bone of contention. However, it is an important area and must be understood.

Dividends

- A £2,000 tax free dividend allowance from April 6th 2020
- Dividends above this level are taxed at 7.5% (basic rate), 32.5% (higher rate), and 38.1% (additional rate)
- Dividends received by pensions and ISAs are unaffected
- Dividend income are treated as the top band of income.
- Individuals who are basic rate payers who receive dividends of more than £2000 will complete self assessment returns.

It doesn't matter whether you get dividends from a company, unit trusts or open-ended investment company, as all dividends are taxed the same way.

How dividends are paid

- When you get your dividend you also get a voucher that shows:

- the dividend paid - the amount you received
- the amount of associated 'tax credit' - see next section

If you have agreed to get your dividends paid electronically you may get your dividend voucher in paper or electronic form.

Capital Gains Tax-What you pay it on

You may have to pay Capital Gains Tax if you make a profit ('gain') when you sell (or 'dispose of') shares or other investments. Shares and investments you may need to pay tax on include:

- shares that aren't in an ISA or PEP
- units in a unit trust
- certain bonds (not including Premium Bonds and Qualifying Corporate Bonds)

You'll need to work out your gain to find out whether you need to pay tax. This will depend on if your total gains are above your Capital Gains Tax allowance for the tax year. Currently in 2020/2021 this is £12,300 for individuals and ££6150 for trusts.

When you don't pay it

You don't usually need to pay tax if you give shares as a gift to your husband, wife, civil partner or a charity. You also don't pay Capital Gains Tax when you dispose of:

- shares you've put into an ISA or PEP
- shares in employer Share Incentive Plans (SIPs)
- UK government gilts (including Premium Bonds)
- Qualifying Corporate Bonds
- employee shareholder shares - depending on when you got them

For more detailed information concerning shares and taxation go to https://www.gov.uk/tax-sell-shares.

**

Ch. 13

Pensions and Planning for the Future

Planning for the future

The main principle with all pension provision is that the sooner you start saving money in a pension plan the more you will have at retirement. The later that you leave it the less you will have or the more expensive that it will be to create a fund adequate enough for your needs.

In order to gauge your retirement needs, you will need to have a clear idea of your lifestyle, or potential lifestyle in retirement. This is not something that you can plan, or want to plan, at a younger age but the main factor is that the more that you have the easier life will be. There are two main factors which currently underpin retirement:

- Improved health and longevity-we are living longer and we have better health so therefore we are more active
- People are better off-improved state and company pensions

Sources of pension and other retirement income

Government statistics indicate that there is a huge gap between the poorest and richest pensioners in the United Kingdom. No surprise there. The difference between the richest fifth of single pensioners and the poorest fifth is about £400 per week. The poorest fifth of pensioners in the UK are reliant mainly on state benefits whilst the wealthier groups have occupational incomes and also personal investment incomes. The outline below indicates sources of pension and also the disparity between the richest and poorest socio-economic groups:

The Pensioners Income Series

The Pensioners' Incomes (PI) Series contains estimates of the levels, sources and distribution of pensioners' incomes. It also examines the position of pensioners within the income distribution of the population as a whole. This can be found at:

www.gov.uk/government/collections/pensioners-incomes-series.

Average income of pensioners

The figures show that the current median weekly income for single pensioners is £285 (2019/20, down from £312 in the 2012-13 tax year. Income earned by retired workers is made up of several sources including the state pension, workplace pensions, personal pensions and income from savings and investments.

Pensioners need £33,000 for a comfortable retirement moneyfacts.co.uk In order for workers to enjoy a comfortable retirement that includes holidays abroad, a generous clothing allowance and a car they will need to have saved enough for a £33,000 per year income.

Couples tend to have more retirement income than single people. Some reports even suggest that in 2017/18, retired couples received more than twice the income of single retirees. This may partly be due to the fact that housing costs were included in the study – couples sharing housing will generally have lower overheads than someone on their own.

Another factor may be that those who are single upon entering retirement are likely to be divorced or separated, which may have had a significant impact on their past finances and thus their ability to save for retirement. People in long-term stable relationships may have a greater capacity for building up retirement funds, as well as a stronger motivation for doing so.

Sources of pensioner incomes

Nearly all pensioners (97 per cent) were in receipt of the State Pension in 2019/20. Income-related benefits were received by a quarter of all pensioners in 2019/20. The percentage of pensioners in receipt of income-related benefits has decreased from 34 per cent in 2005/06 to 25 per cent in 2019/21. This has been influenced by the increase in the State Pension and the targeting of Pension Credit on the pensioners on lowest incomes.

There has been little change in the percentage of pensioners with income from disability benefits. This income category covers a range of benefits paid to individuals as a result of their disability status.

Personal pensions provide income to a smaller group of pensioners than occupational pensions. The percentage of pensioners in receipt has increased over a 10 year period. In 2019/20, 18 per cent of pensioners were in receipt of income from personal pensions, compared with 12 per cent in 2005/06. Recently retired pensioners were more likely to be in receipt than older pensioners, which reflects the relatively recent expansion in the numbers contributing to personal pensions. Personal pensions in their current form were introduced in 1988.

Private pension income includes all non-State Pension

income. Over the past 10 years, there has been an increase in the percentage of pensioners receiving income from private pensions – from 66 per cent to 70 per cent. Investment income was the third most common source of income, received by 63 per cent of all pensioners in 2019/20 although the percentage of pensioners in receipt of investment income has decreased from 70 per cent over the past 10 years. Overall 17 per cent of pensioners were in receipt of earnings. Some of the results for pensioner couples include earnings from one person being under State Pension age.

Pensioners income according to position-bottom fifth of pensioners and top fifth

Benefit income, including State Pension income, was the largest source of income for both single pensioners and couples in the bottom fifth of the income distribution. For pensioner couples in this group benefit income accounted for 78 per cent of their income, while for single pensioners this was 86 per cent. Benefit income made up more than half of all income for all but the top fifth of single pensioners.

For the top fifth of both couples and singles, the largest source of income was from private pension income (38 per cent for couples and 44 per cent for singles). For couples the proportion of income from earnings was highest in the top fifth of the income distribution.

Amongst other things, the above illustrates that those in the poorest and wealthiest bands have a wide gap in income, in particular in the areas of earnings and investments. The richest have managed to ensure that there is enough money in the pot to cater for retirement. Those in the lower income bands rely heavily on state pensions and other benefits. The

Pensioners Income Series measures those within the bottom, middle and top fifth of the population.

How Much Income is needed in Retirement-Planning Ahead

When attempting to forecast for future pension needs, there are a number of factors which need to be taken into account:

These are:

- Your income needs in retirement and how much of that income you can expect to derive from state pensions
- How much pension that any savings you have will produce
- How long you have to save for
- Projected inflation

Income needs in retirement

This is very much a personal decision and will be influenced by a number of factors, such as ongoing housing costs, care costs, projected lifestyle etc. The main factor is that you have enough to live on comfortably. In retirement you will probably take more holidays and want to enjoy your free time. This costs money so your future planning should take into account all your projected needs and costs. When calculating future needs, all sources of income should be taken into account.

What period to save over

The obvious fact is that, the longer period that you save over the more you will build up and hence the more that you will have in retirement. As time goes on savings are compounded and the value of the pot goes up. One thing is for certain and that is if you leave it too late then you will have to put away a large slice of your income to produce a decent pension. If you plan to retire at an early age then you will need to save more to produce the same benefits.

Inflation

As prices rise, so your money buys you less. This is the main effect of inflation and to maintain the same level of spending power you will need to save more as time goes on. Many forms of retirement plans will include a calculation for inflation. Currently, inflation is at a relatively low level, 1.8% per annum (January 2017). However, history shows that the effects of inflation can be corrosive, having risen above 25% per annum in the past. Hopefully, this is now under control

For most people, retirement is a substantial part of life, probably lasting a couple of decades or more. It follows that ensuring your financial security in retirement requires some forward planning. Developing a plan calls for a general review of your current finances and careful consideration of how you can build up your savings to generate the retirement income that you need.

There are five distinct stages to planning your retirement which are summarised below.

Stage 1-this involves checking first that other aspects of your basic finances are in good shape. Planning for retirement generally means locking away your money for a long time. Once invested it is usually impossible to get pension savings back early, even in an emergency. It is therefore essential that you have other more accessible savings available for emergencies and that you do not have any problem debts that could tip you into a financial crisis. You must then weigh up saving for retirement against other goals that are more pressing, such as making sure that your household would be financially secure if you were unable to work because of illness or the main breadwinner dies.

Stage 2-You need to decide how much income you might need when you retire. There is a table overleaf which might help you in calculating this.

Stage 3- Check how much pension that you have built up so far.

Stage 4-Compare your amount from stage 3 with your target income from stage 2.

Stage 5-Review your progress once a year and/or if your circumstances change.

It is a fact that many people need far less in retirement than when actively working. The expenses that exist when working, such as mortgage payments, children and work related expenses do not exist when retired. The average household between 30-49 spends £473 per week and £416 between 50-64. This drops to £263 per week between 65 to 74 and even lower in later retirement (Expenditure and Food Survey).

However, as might be expected, expenditure on health care increases correspondingly with age. Whilst the state may help with some costs the individual still has to bear a high proportion of expenditure on health related items. When calculating how much money you will need in retirement, it is useful to use a table in order to list your anticipated expenses as follows

Everyday needs

Item	Annual Total
Food and other	
Leisure (newspapers etc)	
Pets	
Clothes	
Other household items	
Gardening	
General expenses	

Home expenses

Mortgage/rent	
Service charges/repairs	
Insurance	
Council tax	
Water and other utilities	
Telephone	
TV licence other charges (satellite)	
Other expenses (home help)	

Leisure and general entertainment

Hobbies	
Eating out	
Cinema/theatre	
Holidays	
Other luxuries (smoking/drinking	

Transport

Car expenses	
Car hire	

Petrol etc	
Bus/train fares	

Health

Dental charges	
Optical expenses	
Medical insurance	
Care insurance	
Other health related expenses	

Anniversaries/birthdays etc

Children/grandchildren	
Relatives other than children	
Christmas	
Charitable donations	
Other expenses	

Savings and loans

General savings	
Saving for later retirement	
Other savings	
Loan repayments	

Other

The above should give you an idea of the amounts that you will need per annum to live well. Obviously, you should plan for a monthly income that will meet those needs. You should also take account of income tax on your retirement incomes.

The impact of inflation

When you are planning for many years ahead, it is essential to take account of the effects of inflation. Currently, at the time of writing in 2020, we are in a period of relatively low inflation, 0.3% largely due to low oil prices. As prices rise over the years, the money we will have will buy less and less. For example, in the extreme case, if prices double then a fixed amount of money will buy only half as much. The higher the rate of inflation, the more you have to save to reach your income target.

Some pension schemes give you automatic protection against inflation, but many don't and it is largely up to you to decide what protection to build into your planning. The first step is to be aware what effect inflation might have. Fortunately, pension statements and projections these days must all be adjusted for inflation so that figures you are given are expressed in today's money. This gives you an idea of the standard of living you might expect and helps you assess the amount that you need to save. Providers of non-pension investments (such as unit trusts and investment trusts (see later chapters) do not have to give you statements and projections adjusted for inflation. If you use these other investments for your retirement then you will have to make your own adjustments.

If you require more detailed forecasting you should go to www.ons.gov.uk (Office of National Statistics).

In the next chapters we will be discussing the various sources of pensions, starting with the all-important State Pension.

**

Ch. 14

Sources of Pensions-A Summary

The state pension

Over 96% of single pensioners and 99% of couples receive the basic state pension. Therefore, it is here to stay. Everyone who has paid the appropriate national insurance contributions will be entitled to a state pension. If you are not working you can either receive pension credits, as discussed, or make voluntary contributions.

The full (basic) state pension is £134.24 for a single person (2020) From April 2020, for men who were born after 6th April 1951 and women who were born after 6th April 1953 the pension is £175.18 per week. This is known as a 'flat rate' or 'single tier' system and is designed to make the current system more simple and easier to understand. Getting the flat rate however, is very much dependant on contributions.

Basic state pensions are increased each April in line with price inflation. State pensioners also receive a (£10 Christmas bonus-check current entitlement) and are entitled to winter fuel payments. Married women can claim a pension based on their spouse's NI record. Men who have reached 65 are also able to claim a basic state pension based on their wife's contribution record where the wife reaches state pension age on or after 6th April 2010.

Same sex couples, as a result of the Civil Partnerships Act

2004, along with married couples of the same sex, following the passing of the Marriage (Same sex Couples Act) 2014, have the same rights as heterosexual couples in all aspects of pension provision.

Transsexual people

Your State Pension might be affected if you're a transsexual person and you:

- were born between 24 December 1919 and 3 April 1945
- were claiming State Pension before 4 April 2005
- can provide evidence that your gender reassignment surgery took place before 4 April 2005

You don't need to do anything if you legally changed your gender and started claiming State Pension on or after 4 April - you'll already be claiming based on your legal gender. For more details go to www.gov.uk/state-pension/eligibility

How many qualifying years do you need to get the full State Pension?

The number of qualifying years you need to get a full state pension depends on when you reach your State Pension age. If you reached State Pension age before 6 April 2010, you normally needed 44 qualifying years if you are a man, or 39 qualifying years if you are woman. If you reach State Pension age on or after 6 April 2010 but before 6 April 2016, you need 30 qualifying years. If you reach State Pension age on or after 6 April 2016, you normally need 35 qualifying years.

Using someone else's contribution record

In some circumstances, you may be able to use your husband's, wife's or civil partner's contribution record to help you qualify for a State Pension.

Pension credits

Pension credits began life in October 2003. The credit is designed to top up the resources of pensioners whose income is low. The pension credit has two components: a guarantee credit and a saving credit.

The Guarantee credit

This is available to anyone over a qualifying age (equal to women's state pension age-see further on) whose income is less than a set amount called the minimum guarantee. The guarantee will bring income up to £173.75 for a single person and £265.20 for a couple (including civil partners and same sex couples) (2020-2021). The minimum guarantee is higher for certain categories of disabled people and carers. The qualifying age for Pension Credit is gradually going up to 66 in line with the increase in the State Pension age for women to 65 and the further increase to 66 for men and women.

The Savings credit

You can only claim savings credit if you or your partner are aged 65 or over. It's intended as a modest "reward" if you've provided yourself with a retirement income over and above the basic retirement pension.Savings credit is calculated by the The maximum savings credit you can get is £13.97 a week if you're single and £15.62 a week if you're married or living with a partner.

The income taken into account for savings credit is the same as for guarantee credit, but various types of income are now ignored. These are Working Tax Credit, contribution-based Employment and Support Allowance, Incapacity Benefit, contribution-based Jobseeker's Allowance, Severe Disablement Allowance, Maternity Allowance and maintenance payments made to you (child maintenance is always ignored).

If your income is still over the savings threshold, the Pension Service works out your entitlement to savings credit.

If you reach State Pension age on or after 6 April 2016

Most people who reach State Pension age on or after 6 April 2016 won't be eligible for Savings Credit. But you may continue to get Savings Credit if both of the following apply:

- you're in a couple and one of you reached State Pension age before 6 April 2016
- you were getting Savings Credit up to 6 April 2016

If you stop being eligible for Savings Credit for any reason from 6 April 2016, you won't be able to get it again.

National Insurance Credits

In some situations you may get National Insurance Credits, which plug what would otherwise be gaps in your NI record. You might get credits in the following situations:

- when you are unemployed, or unable to work   because you are ill, and claiming certain benefits

- If you were aged 16 to 18 before 6 April 2010, you were usually credited automatically with National Insurance credits. No new awards will be made from 6 April 2010.
- if you are on an approved training course
- when you are doing jury service
- if you are getting Statutory Adoption Pay, Statutory Maternity Pay, Additional Statutory Paternity Pay, Statutory Sick Pay, Maternity Allowance or Working Tax Credit
- if you have been wrongly put in prison
- if you are caring for a child or for someone who is sick or disabled
- if you are aged 16 or over and provided care for a child under 12, that you are related to and you lived in the UK for the period(s) of care
- if your spouse or civil partner is a member of Her Majesty's forces and you are accompanying them on an assignment outside the UK

There are special arrangements for people who worked or were detained without pay in Iraq during the Gulf Crisis. If you think you might be affected by this, write to HM Revenue & Customs (HMRC) at: HM Revenue & Customs
National Insurance Contributions & Employer Office
Benton Park View, Newcastle upon Tyne
NE98 1ZZ
Tel: 0300 200 3211
The State Pension age

Currently, the state pension age is 66 for men and women. There will be further increases in the state pension age to 68 for men and women. The increase in the State Pension age is being phased in and your own particular pension age depends on when you were born. The proposed changes affect people born between April 1953 and 5th April 1960. (For your own retirement age you should go to the Pensions Service Website).

Additional state pension
S2P replaced the State Earnings Related Pension (SERPS) in April 2002. SERPS was, essentially, a state second tier pension and it was compulsory to pay into this in order to supplement the basic state pension. There were drawbacks however, and many people fell through the net so S2P was introduced to allow other groups to contribute. S2P refined SERPS allowing the following to contribute:

- People caring for children under six and entitled to child benefit
- Carers looking after someone who is elderly or disabled, if they are entitled to carers allowance
- Certain people who are unable to work because of illness or disability, if they are entitled to long-term incapacity benefit or severe disablement allowance and they have been in the workforce for at least one-tenth of their working life
- Self-employed people are excluded from S2P as are employees earning less than the lower earnings limit. Married women and widows paying class 1 contributions at the reduced rate do not build up additional state pension.

S2P is an earnings related scheme. This means that people on high earnings build up more pension than those on lower earnings. However, people earning at least the lower earnings limit are treated as if they have earnings at that level and so build up more pension than they otherwise would.

Contracting out

A person does not build up state additional pension during periods when they are contracted out. Contracting out means that a person has opted to join an occupational scheme or a personal pensions scheme or stakeholder pension. While contacted out, a person will pay lower National Insurance Contributions on part of earnings or some of the contributions paid by an employee and employer are 'rebated' and paid into the occupational pension scheme or other pension scheme.

Increasing your state pension

There are a number of ways in which you can increase your State Pension, particularly if you have been presented with a pension forecast which shows lack of contributions and a diminished state pension. You can fill gaps in your pension contributions or you can defer your state pension. HM Revenue and Customs have a help line on 0300 200 3300 to check your record and to receive advice on whether you have gaps and how to fill them.

Filling gaps in your record

If you wish to plug gaps in your contributions, normally you can go back 6 years to fill gaps in your record. However, if you will reached State Pension Age before April 5th 2015, special rules let you fill any gaps up to six years in total going back as far as 6th April 1975. You can make class 3 contributions to fill the gap, each contribution costs £15.30 so a full years worth costs 52 times £15.30 = £795.60). Making class three contributions can't increase your additional state pension. However Class 3 contributions do count towards the state bereavement benefits that your wife, husband or civil partner could claim if you were to die.

Deferring your state pension

Another way to boost your state pension is to delay its commencement. You can put off drawing your pension for as long as you like, there is no time limit. You must defer your whole pension, including any additional or graduated pensions and you earn an addition to the lump sum or a bigger cash sum.

In the past, if you put off drawing your own pension and your wife was getting a pension based on your NI record, her pension would also have to be deferred and she would have to agree to this. From 6th April 2010 onwards, husbands and civil partners as well as wives may be able to claim a pension based on their partners record. But a change to the rules now means that, if you defer your pension and your wife, husband or civil partner claims on your record, they no longer have to defer their pension as well. If your pension has already started to be paid, you can decide to stop payments in order to earn extra pension or lump sum. But you can only defer your pension once. You can earn an increase in the pension when it does start of 1% for every five weeks you put off the pension. This is equivalent to an increase of 10.4% for each whole year.

Alternatively, if you put off claiming your pension for at least a whole year, you can earn a one-off lump sum instead of extra pension. The lump sum is taxable but only at the top rate you were paying before getting the lump sum. Whatever the size of the sum it does not mean that you move tax brackets.   The Pension Service, which is part of the Department of Work and Pensions publishes a detailed guide to deferring your State pension. Go to www. gov.uk-contact-pension-service.

Women and Pensions

It is a general rule that women pensioners tend to have less income than their male counterparts. Therefore, when building a retirement plan, women need to consider what steps they and their partners can take to make their financial future more secure.

Particular issues for women

These days, the rules of any particular pension scheme-whether state or private, do not discriminate between men and women. Whether male or female you pay the same to access the same level of benefits. However, this does not always mean that women end up with the same level of pension as men. This is because of the general working and lifestyle differences between men and women, for example women are more likely to take breaks from work and take part time work so they can look after family. As a result, women are more likely to pay less into a pension fund than men.

Historically, the (idealised) role of women as carers was built into the UK pensions system. Not least the state pension system.

It was assumed that women would marry before having children and rely on their husbands to provide for them financially right through to retirement. As a result, women who have already retired typically have much lower incomes than men. Changes to the state scheme for people reaching state pension age from 6th April 2010 onwards, mean that most women will, in future, retire with similar state pensions as men. However if you are an unmarried women living with a partner you should be aware of the following:

The state scheme recognises wives, husbands and civil partners but not unmarried partners. This means that if your unmarried partner dies before you, you would not be eligible for the state benefits that provide support for bereaved dependants.

Occupational schemes and personal pensions typically pay survivor benefits to a bereaved partner, whether married or not. However many schemes-especially in the public sector-have recognised unmarried partners only recently and, as a result, the survivor pension for an unmarried partner may be very low.

The legal system recognises that wives, husbands and civil partners may have a claim on retirement savings built up by the other party in the event of divorce, but these will be considered along with all the other assets to be split between you and you may end up with a much lower retirement income than you had been expecting.

The legal system does not give similar rights to unmarried partners who split up. If your unmarried partner was building up pension savings for you both, he or she can walk away with all those savings and you have no legal claim on them.

Effects of changes to the state pension from 2016 on women

As we have discussed, from April 2020, the new "flat rate " state pension will typically be £175.20 a week, but only for those who have paid national insurance contributions (NIC's) for 35 years. Many women will not qualify, having taken career breaks to care for children.

If there are gaps in your entitlement then consider buying some added years of state pension which you can do in the run-up to retirement. The state pension purchase scheme is far more generous than any private pension, provided you live more than a few years in retirement. Be careful, though, that you're not going to be buying years that you'd actually make up through work between now and retirement, otherwise you could end up giving the government money for something you'd have got anyway. Voluntary NIC's cost £15.30 a week or £795.60 a year, and you can normally fill gaps from the past six years. If you are due to retire after April 2016, check to see how much you will receive at gov.uk/future-pension-centre.

Have you told the government you are a carer?

The good news is that full-time unpaid carers will be entitled to the same pension as those who have worked in a paid full-time job from 2016. However, thousands of women who do not claim child benefit or carers' allowance could miss out.

These benefits signal to the Department for Work and Pensions (DWP) that an individual qualifies for NIC's. Since households earning above £50,000 are no longer eligible to claim full child benefit, and those earning over £60,000 will receive no child benefit at all, many stay-at home mums may go under the radar. Similarly if women are caring for a family member but not claiming carer's allowance their unpaid work will go unrecognised. If you are a carer but don't claim any benefits pro-actively contact the DWP to report your situation.

If your household income is over £50,000 but under £60,000 you should still register for child benefit in order to receive NIC's.

The over 80 pension

This is a non-contributory pension for people aged 80 or over with little or no state pension. If you are 80 or over, not getting or getting a reduced state pension because you have not paid enough National Insurance contributions (NI) and are currently living in England, Scotland or Wales and have been doing so for a total of 10 years or more in any continuous period of 20 years before or after your 80th birthday, you could claim the over 80 pension. The maximum amount of the over 80 state pension that you can get is currently £73.30 per week (2017/18).

Occupational pensions

Briefly, occupational pension schemes are a very important source of income. With Occupational pension schemes the contract is between the company and the pension provider. With Group Personal Pension Schemes, which we will also be discussing later, although the employer chooses the company the contract is between the employee and the pension company.

Occupational pension Schemes are one of the best ways to pay into a pension scheme as the employer has to contribute a significant amount to the pot. Over the years the amounts paid into occupational pension schemes has increased significantly.

Although there have been a number of incidences of occupational schemes being wound up this is relatively small and they remain a key source of retirement income.

From October 2012, it has been compulsory for employers to provide an occupational pension scheme, Auto Enrolment. For the first time, employers are obliged to:

enrol most of their workforce into a pension scheme; and
make employer pension contributions

This will affect all employers in the UK, regardless of the number of individuals that they employ. Anyone who is classed as a 'worker' for National Minimum Wage purposes is included in the new pension regime.

This will be introduced in stages, and each employer will be given a 'staging date' determined by how many employees they had as at April 1st 2012.

Stakeholder schemes

Stakeholder pension schemes are designed for those people who do not have an employer, or had an employer who did not have an occupational scheme. They therefore cannot pay into an occupational scheme. If an employer did not offer an occupational scheme (many small employers were exempt) they had to arrange access to a stakeholder scheme. Employees did not have to join an occupational scheme offered by employers, instead they could join a stakeholder scheme. Likewise, self-employed people can also join a stakeholder scheme.

Stakeholder schemes have a contribution limit-this being

currently £3,600 per year. Anyone who is not earning can also pay into a scheme, up to the limit above. You pay money to a pension provider (eg an insurance company, bank or building society) who invests it (eg in shares).These are a type of personal pension but they have to meet some minimum standards set by the government. These include:

- management charges can't be more than 1.5% of the fund's value for the first 10 years and 1% after that
- you must be able to start and stop payments when you want or switch providers without being charged
- they have to meet certain security standards, eg have independent trustees and auditors.

How much can be invested in a stakeholder pension?

There is no limit to the amount that can be invested in a stakeholder pension scheme. However, tax relief can only be obtained on contributions up to a maximum annual contribution limit (known as an individual's 'annual allowance'). For the tax year 2020/21, this is set at the lower of 100% of an individual's UK earnings or £40,000 per annum. Carry forward of unused allowances may be permitted in some circumstances. It is possible to contribute up to £4,000 per year (including tax relief) into a stakeholder pension scheme even if a person is not earning. A member of an occupational pension scheme may also contribute to a stakeholder pension scheme. You can start making payments into a stakeholder pension from £20 per month. You can pay weekly or monthly. If you don't want to make regular payments you can pay lump sums any time you want.

The rules for stakeholder pensions changed on 1 October 2012. If you're starting a new job now or returning to one, your employer doesn't have to offer you access to a stakeholder pension scheme. They now have to offer entry through automatic enrolment. If you're in a stakeholder pension scheme that was arranged by your employer before 1 October 2012, they must continue to take and pay contributions from your wages. This arrangement is in place until:

- you ask them to stop
- you stop paying contributions at regular intervals
- you leave your job

If you leave your job or change to another personal pension, the money they have paid in stays in your pension pot unless you have it transferred to a different pension provider.

Other ways to save for retirement

The government offers certain tax advantages to encourage pension saving. However, the most advantageous savings plan is the Individual Savings Account (ISA) discussed previously. In addition, you might have regular savings accounts, your home or a second home. All of these possibilities must be factored in when arriving at an adequate retirement income.

**

Useful addresses and websites

Association of Investment Companies (AIC)
9th Floor
24 Chiswell Street
London EC1Y 4YY
Hotline: 020 7282 5555
www.theaic.co.uk

Debt Management Office
Eastcheap Court
11 Philpot Lane
London EC3M 8UD
www.dmo.gov.uk

Financial Ombudsman Service (FOS)
Consumer helpline: 0800 023 4 567
www.financial-ombudsman.org,uk

Financial Conduct Authority (FCA)
25 The North Colonnade
Canary Wharf
London E14 5HS
Consumer helpline: 0800 111 6768
www.fca.org.uk

HMRC.gov.uk
Matters relating to all tax queries

International Pension Centre
Tel: 01912 187777
(8.00am-8.00pm,weekdays)

Investment Association
Camomile Court
23 Camomile Street
London EC3A 7LL
0207 831 0898

MoneyFACTS
www.moneyfacts.co.uk

The Pension Service
www.thepensionservice.gov.uk

Pension Advisory Service
(TPAS)
11 Belgrave Road
London SW1V 1RB
Helpline: 0300 123 1047
www.pensionsadvisoryservice.org.uk

Trade Bodies
The Investment Association
Camomile Court
23 Camomile Street
London EC3A 7LL
0207 831 0898

Proshare Investment Clubs
5th Floor
10 Lower Thames Street
London EC3R 6AD
0203 657 7700
www.proshare.org.uk

The Association of British Insurers
One America Square
17 Crosswall
London EC3N 2LB
020 7600 3333
www.abi.org.uk

The British Insurance Brokers Association
John Stow House
18 Bevis Marks
London EC3A 7JB
0344 7700 266-www.biba.org.uk

UK Finance,
5th Floor, One Angel Court
30 Throgmorton Street
London, EC2R 7HJ
www.ukfinance.org.uk

Borrowing
The National Debtline-0808 808 4000
www.nationaldebtline.co.uk

The Association of British Credit Unions Limited

Holyoake House
Hanover Street
Manchester M60 OAS
0161 832 3694
www.abcul.org

Credit Information Agencies
Experian

https://ins.experian.co.uk

Equifax Europe (UK)

www.equifax.co.uk

**

Index

**